William Morton Payne

Little leaders

William Morton Payne

Little leaders

ISBN/EAN: 9783743322189

Manufactured in Europe, USA, Canada, Australia, Japa

Cover: Foto ©Thomas Meinert / pixelio.de

Manufactured and distributed by brebook publishing software (www.brebook.com)

William Morton Payne

Little leaders

LITTLE LEADERS

BY

WILLIAM MORTON PAYNE

CHICAGO
WAY & WILLIAMS
1895

COPYRIGHT
BY WAY AND WILLIAMS
MDCCCXCV

TO MY OLD FRIEND AND FELLOW-WORKER

FRANCIS FISHER BROWNE

WHO HAS DONE MORE THAN ANY OTHER
MAN TO PROMOTE THE INTERESTS
OF LITERATURE IN
CHICAGO

PREFACE.

THE contents of this little book consist of a series of papers reprinted from 'The Dial,' in which periodical, scattered through the past three years, they first did duty as editorial articles. The title now given to the collection is thus accounted for, as well as the use of the plural pronoun, which it seemed best to retain. The papers make no pretence of doing more than touch the skirts and fringes of the great subjects with which they are concerned, and whatever readers they may reach are asked to bear this fact indulgently in mind. They are reproduced substantially as they appeared, with but trifling alterations. Two of them, it should be added, have been incorporated into the introduction of the book 'English in American Universities,' edited by their author, and very recently published.

CHICAGO, November 1, 1895.

CONTENTS.

LITERATURE AND CRITICISM.

SONNET — *Ej Blot til Lyst.*

	PAGE
LITERATURE ON THE STAGE	13
THE IBSEN LEGEND	23
THE CULT IN LITERATURE	31
THE LITERARY WEST	40
THE WRITER AND HIS HIRE	49
THE CRITIC AND HIS TASK	56
TOUCHSTONES OF CRITICISM	62
ANONYMITY IN LITERARY CRITICISM	71
POETRY AS CRITICISM OF LITERATURE	81
THE NEGLECTED ART OF TRANSLATION	90

EDUCATION.

SONNET — *The Higher Aim.*

A FEW WORDS ABOUT EDUCATION	101
THE APPROACH TO LITERATURE	109
THE TEACHING OF LITERATURE	117
DEMOCRACY AND EDUCATION	127
THE FUTURE OF AMERICAN SPEECH	136
THE USE AND ABUSE OF DIALECT	146

CONTENTS—*Continued.*

	PAGE
READING AND EDUCATION	155
SUMMER READING	163
THE SUMMER SCHOOL	169
AN ENDOWED NEWSPAPER	178

IN MEMORIAM.
SONNET — *Conservation.*

ALFRED TENNYSON	189
ERNEST RENAN	200
HIPPOLYTE ADOLPHE TAINE	209
GUSTAV FREYTAG	220
JOHN ADDINGTON SYMONDS	229
CHRISTINA GEORGINA ROSSETTI	237
JOHN TYNDALL	246
THOMAS HENRY HUXLEY	255
OLIVER WENDELL HOLMES	264
WILLIAM FREDERICK POOLE	270

LITERATURE AND CRITICISM

'EJ BLOT TIL LYST.'

[These words, meaning 'Not for pleasure only,' are inscribed above the stage of the Royal Theatre at Copenhagen.]

NOT merely for our pleasure, but to purge
   The soul from baseness, from ignoble fear,
   And all the passions that make dim the clear
Calm vision of the world; our feet to urge
On to ideal far-set goals; to merge
     Our being with the heart of things; brought near
   The springs of life, to make us see and hear
And feel its swelling and pulsating surge:—

Such, Thespian art divine, thy nobler aim;
   For this the tale of Œdipus was told,
   Of frenzied Lear, Harpagon's greed of gold;—
And, knowing this, how must we view with shame
   Thy low estate, and hear the plaudits loud
   That mark thee now but pander to the crowd!

LITERATURE ON THE STAGE.

THERE has been of late, both in England and America, one of the periodically recurrent outbursts of criticism and discussion of the English-speaking stage, its present degradation, and its possible future redemption. Attention has been called, in all possible tones of indignation, to the old familiar facts; to the evils of the 'star' system, to the alarming prominence of the spectacular element in dramatic production, and to the insistence of the public upon being amused, at whatever cost of the artistic proprieties. That all these evils exist, and many more, is evident to the most casual observer. The theatrical records of London, New York, and Chicago, alike give evidence of a noble art degenerated into a mere amusement, and of the almost complete severance of literature from the stage. But talking about these evils is not likely to prove effective in removing them. The talking will be done by a few earnest people, and the unthinking masses will give, as before, the sanction of their support to the dramatic monstrosities that chiefly occupy our stage. Discussion of the subject but supplies, after all, a new illustration of the homely saying that 'a watched pot never boils'; in other words, the kingdom of true dramatic art, like a certain other kingdom, cometh not with observation. The great periods of the art, when literture securely trod the stage, did not result from a deliberate and reasoned conclusion that such art was a desirable possession, but were the spontaneous product of a heightened national consciousness seeking for adequate expression. Such expression was found in the ages and countries of Pericles and of Louis Quatorze, in the period of Spanish history that culminated with the glories of Calderon and Lope de Vega, and at the time of that vast expansion of the English spirit which produced Marlowe and Webster and Shakespeare. We may well wonder what manner of men they were who flocked to their rude theatres in 'the spacious times of great Elizabeth,' and shared, with no adventitious spectacular allurements to serve as a fillip, in the pure intellectual delight offered by 'The Tempest' or 'A Midsummer

Night's Dream.' As Mr. Symonds says, 'There remains always something inscrutable in the spontaneous efforts of a nation finely touched to a fine issue.'

The stage of to-day certainly does not give us, in England and America, any indication of 'a nation finely touched to a fine issue.' The playwright, not the poet, the contriver of puppets, not the creator of characters, occupies the higher plane of our existing dramatic art, while the lower plane is hopelessly given over to the buffoon, who acts after his kind. The situation is much better upon the continent of Europe, for there, at least, the stage has an unbroken and dignified tradition. If it can boast few living writers of great distinction, it still preserves its character as a school of conscientious acting, of correct diction, and of accurate enunciation. As a conservator of the national speech the Théâtre Français is as important and influential a body as the Académie Française, while a similar function is fulfilled by the theatres of many German cities and of the Scandinavian capitals. To realize what this means, we have only to imagine the derision that would greet the proposal to decide some disputed question of English style or pronunciation by reference to the practise of the stage in any English or American city. The explanation of this difference is, of course, largely political. The chief European governments have always held the stage to be an educational institution, and, as such, a legitimate object of government support. The noble motto of the Danish national theatre has been made the working rule of the government-aided European stage. The Théâtre Français permits no week to pass without performance of some work by Corneille, Racine, or Molière; the court theatres of Austria and Germany as frequently produce the plays of Lessing and Schiller, of Goethe and Shakespeare. But in no theatre of the English-speaking world is the presentation of Shakespearian drama thus made a matter of fixed weekly or even monthly recurrence. Germany pays more reverence than we do to our own dramatic poet, to the chief glory of all dramatic literature.

One might suppose that this neglect of a great art would have long since led to the disappearance of the drama from our literature. But the essential vitality of the dramatic form, and the inherent fitness of our English speech to assume that mode of expression, have given us, in spite of all discouragements, an almost unbroken succession of noble dramatic poems. Although our century refuses to witness stage productions of the great works of English dramatic literature, and although they are denied the support of even the reading public, they are still produced in numbers, for the instinct of the poet well knows the value of dramatic expression, and he will not abandon it, however the public may scorn the product of his labors. Such poems as 'The Cenci' of Shelley and the 'Count Julian' of Landor, or the plays of Browning and Mr. Swinburne, had they been written by Frenchmen or Germans, would not have had to wait long before taking their proper places in the classic repertory of the stage. And the greatest poet of our own age, had he not been English, would have obtained more than a grudging recognition, as fitted for stage purposes, of but one or two of the magnificent series of his historical and romantic dramas. Had a German poet written 'Harold' and 'Becket,' or a French poet written 'The Foresters,' these works would have had more than a cold *succès d'estime*, for they would have reached a public quick to recognize literary excellence in the drama, and prompt to express its approval of noble workmanship. In excellent dramatic work of a rank lower than the first, our nineteenth century literature is also rich, and to a degree which few readers and no mere theatre-goers suspect. Such plays as Sergeant Talfourd's 'Ion' and Dean Milman's 'Fazio,' both of which once had a precarious tenure of the stage, well deserve to be revived; the dramatic poems of Sir Henry Taylor, Richard Hengist Horne, and Westland Marston, are infinitely more deserving of attention than nine-tenths of the plays actually produced upon our stage. But they would be caviare to the general audience, hopelessly dull in appreciation of style, and trained to prefer buffoonery to comedy, melodrama to tragedy, or, at the very best, sentiment to passion.

The almost complete severance of literature from the English stage is clearly enough shown by the fact that the dramatic works of Tennyson have never succeeded in gaining a foothold there. If a still more striking illustration is wished, it can be furnished by the experience of the Shelley Society in its attempts to produce 'The Cenci.' According to English law, only licensed plays may be publicly produced. An unlicensed play may be given private performance, a term which means that no money shall be taken at the doors of the theatre, but which is otherwise so conveniently vague that any such performance, arranged in the best of faith, may be undertaken only at considerable risk of violating the law in some unsuspected way. 'The Cenci,' we must add, the greatest English dramatic poem of the century, has been steadily refused a license by the English authorities, although several applications to legalize its performance have been made. In 1886, the Shelley Society gave a private performance of 'The Cenci' in a London theatre, in presence of perhaps the most distinguished audience that recent years have seen collected for any purpose whatever. But the outraged dignity of the censorship was prompt to act, and the manager of the theatre in question was allowed to continue his lease only on condition of never thereafter lending his stage for the production of an unlicensed play. In the centennial year of the birth of Shelley, the Society wished to commemorate the occasion by a repetition of the 'Cenci' performance, but found it impossible either to get the play licensed for public representation, or to find a manager willing to risk lending his theatre for the private performance contemplated. So the plan was abandoned, and a fresh victory scored for the hosts of the Philistine.

When matters reach such a pass as this, it certainly behooves the friends of literature to see if something cannot be done to rehabilitate the stage. It is not a little significant that an Independent Theatre should have been organized in London a few years ago, and that some of the more thoughtful literary men of this country should, at about the same time, have united to establish in New York the Theatre of Arts and Letters. The still older Théâtre Libre of Paris, and the more recent Théâtre de l' Œuvre, might at first seem to deserve mention in this category, but certainly have not resulted from a similar necessity, for French dramatic art needs no such encouragement. But the London and New York organizations adopted what is probably the best method, in a country the genius of whose institutions hardly admits of a stage subsidized by the government, for the furtherance of an important and neglected cause. The untimely collapse of the Theatre of Arts and Letters seems to have resulted rather from bad management than from any fault of the underlying principle. Its programme, and the names of the men who stood sponsors for its plans, promised a serious aim, and the employment of methods consistent with both the dignity of literature and the best dramatic traditions. The most valuable work done by the Independent Theatre of London was the production of several of Dr. Ibsen's dramas of modern society, which certainly represent a tendency in dramatic art deserving of encouragement. Its production of Webster's 'Duchess of Malfy' was another step in the right direction, reminding us that the century which has partly neglected Shakespeare has totally neglected the other men of that great race of Elizabethans above whose level it required the stature of a Shakespeare to tower. The later organization known as the Elizabethan Stage Society, whose object is the presentation of Elizabethan plays under sixteenth century conditions, has also undertaken a work of great educational importance. Last of all, we may mention the recent performance, under the auspices of the English Department of Harvard

University, of Jonson's 'Silent Woman.' The success of this experiment was such as to encourage other colleges to similar undertakings. Both in England and America, we have for many years had the 'Greek Play' and the 'Latin Play,' as occasional features of college work; is not the 'English Play' quite as deserving of attention, even from a strictly educational standpoint?

THE IBSEN LEGEND.

ONE of the most curious chapters of literary history is that which deals with the greatest of Roman poets as he appeared to the imagination of the Middle Ages. The Master Virgil of mediævalism stands out as a vivid enough figure, exerting a marked influence upon the current of mediæval thought; yet how unlike the personality of the Mantuan as he appears to us, with our fuller knowledge of classical times, and the truer intellectual perspective of our view. It was a singular refraction, indeed, that shaped the outlines of the poet into the distorted figure of the wizard, a strange limitation of outlook that in so literal a sense made of his name a word with which to conjure, while blind to his genius and its true significance. Books have their fates, runs the Latin saying, and presumably their authors no less. But never was the fate of bookman more ironical than that of the poet of the 'Æneid' and the 'Fourth Eclogue,' envisaged, a thousand years after his death, as an allegorist and a wonder-worker.

It is a far cry, in more ways than one, from Virgil to Dr. Ibsen, and there is but a single fact that could lead us even for a moment to couple their names. That fact is the prevalence and seemingly continued growth, at least in England and America, of an Ibsen legend, grotesquely divergent from the truth, and calculated to make of the Norwegian poet and dramatist a figure as unlike his real self as Master Virgil was unlike the poet who chiefly made glorious the Augustan Age. Our newspapers, and even some of our serious organs of opinion, afford frequent indications that the popular consciousness holds Dr. Ibsen to be the poet of gloom, of the morbid aspects of character, of the seamy side of life and the unsavory among human relations. A German sensationalist, long discredited, but whose latest work has recently been getting much attention, finds in Dr. Ibsen a conspicuous illustration of what he calls *Entartung*. A typical newspaper article just now under our eye, an article of the better sort and evidently written in all seriousness, calls him 'grim' and 'egotistical,' speaks of his 'icy indifference,' his 'dank philosophy,' and his 'intolerable pessimism.' No one who does much reading in current criticism can have failed more than once to come across even the suggestion that he deliberately panders to the lower instincts of human nature, that he revels in what is revolting and unclean.

Anyone who has read the writings of Dr. Ibson, and who knows something of the aims and ideals that they embody, rubs his eyes in wonderment when he meets with such epithets and opinions as have just been mentioned. But when amazement at the misconception has a little abated, he is apt to ask himself if there is any possible way of accounting for the origin of opinions so grotesque, unless, indeed, he summarily sets them down as adding another to the many existing illustrations of the essential irrationality of the majority of minds. The last count of the indictment above outlined may safely be left to shift for itself. There is no shred of evidence for it, and no sane mind could for a moment seriously entertain the suggestion. Nor is it without reluctance that we so far consider the poet's 'icy indifference' as to recall the infinite tenderness of 'Brand' and 'Peer Gynt,' or illustrate his 'dank philosophy' by the passionate idealism of 'Love's Comedy' and 'Emperor and Galilean.' The reader is to be pitied, indeed, who is not stirred to the depths of his soul by the agonies of Brand as child and wife are taken from him one after the other, or by that vision of the 'third kingdom' which, in the story of Julian, casts its mystical glamour over the last struggle of dying paganism, and which might have been inspired by the choruses of Shelley's 'Hellas.'

The last of these illustrations leads us to the subject upon which more than a word or a reference is needed. Of all the charges commonly made against Dr. Ibsen, that of pessimism is probably the most persistent. This is not surprising when we consider the ignorant way in which that term is bandied about by most people, yet here, if ever, the accusation calls for an energetic protest. Pessimism is both a mood and a philosophical doctrine. Whatever standing it has, considered in its latter aspect, it owes to the authority of Schopenhauer, who, by logic convincing at least to himself, thought he had demonstrated the soul of things to be evil, believed irremediable suffering to lie at the root of conscious existence. To this doctrine the whole of Dr. Ibsen's work is tacitly but resolutely opposed. He never presents to us the gloomy side of life without suggesting the possibility of something better, rarely without indicating the way out of what seems an *impasse* to the soul of little faith. So far from preaching evil as irremediable, he constantly ascribes it to lack of knowledge, infirmity of vision, and weakness of will. If there is any one trait dominant above all others throughout his writings, it is the persistent note of an idealism unshaken by

> 'The absurdity of men,
> Their vaunts, their feats,'

an idealism as absolutely opposed as anything well can be to the philosophical doctrine of pessimism. If Dr. Ibsen is to be styled a pessimist in this sense, it must be in the company of all the satirists, ancient and modern, who have scourged the vices of mankind, and all the moralists who have discerned the good life and sought to bring about its realization in fact no less than in dream.

Of pessimism as a mood it may be said that Dr. Ibsen exhibits it as it has been exhibited by greater men than he, from Homer to Tennyson, by a large proportion, in fact, of the greatest poets that have ever lived. This merely means that he does not, like such men as Browning and Emerson, deliberately exclude from his view a large share of the facts of human life, that he is not content to build for himself a fool's paradise and dwell therein. He is not to be deluded by

> 'The barren optimistic sophistries
> Of comfortable moles,'

and endeavors, according to the light that is in him, to see life steadily and see it whole. Like all writers of the second or third rank, he has his limitations, and his vision is defective; but to describe his prevalent mood as pessimistic, or even as cynical, is grossly to pervert the truth.

The principal reasons for the current misconception of Dr. Ibsen's fundamental attitude towards life may be briefly set forth. In the first place, much of his work is satirical, and this fact, combined with his power of expressing the white heat of indignation, naturally makes many people think that only one at heart a cynic could find so much to condemn in the conduct and the ideals of his fellow-men. In the second place, his work is nearly all dramatic in form, and dramatists always suffer from a more or less unconscious identification with the characters of their own creation, however objectively conceived. Last of all, and most important as far as the English-speaking public is concerned, he unfortunately first became known, and is still chiefly known, by means of a group of his least characteristic and enduring works. Most people get their whole notion of him from a group of three or four plays which deal with extremely narrow and specific social problems, which are utterly inadequate to convey his essential message, and which embody no suggestion of the high poetic energy with which his really great work is charged. It is not altogether surprising that the 'Ibsen legend' should find credence with readers who know only 'A Doll Home,' 'Ghosts,' 'Hedda Gabler,' and 'Solness.' To such, and to all who would know what Dr. Ibsen really stands for, we proffer the advice to read 'Brand' and 'Peer Gynt,' those masterpieces of robust social philosophy and high ethical aim. Their invigorating moral atmosphere has the tonic quality of which our flabby civilization is most in need; their lofty idealism may well put to shame our opportunism, our half-heartedness, and all the paltry conventionalities by which our lives are misshapen. And we venture to say that whoever once takes those works to heart will hardly thereafter describe their author as a pessimist, or talk glibly of his 'icy indifference' and his 'dank philosophy.' For such readers, at least, the 'Ibsen legend' will be at once consigned to the limbo to which grown-up men and women relegate the nursery tales and pious fables that were literally accepted in childhood, but that cannot impose upon the rationalized adult intelligence.

THE CULT IN LITERATURE.

THE great poets are all dead now, and appearances indicate that the twentieth century will begin its course undominated by any commanding figure bequeathed to it from the literature of the nineteenth. No Goethe will loom above that new horizon as in the early dawn of the present century; no Scott is likely to brighten the morning clouds of the new era with the radiance of his genius. We cannot, of course, make any such predictions with absolute confidence that the future will justify them, for the individual manifestations of genius are as incalculable as are the flashings out of new stars, or the appearance within the solar system of unfamiliar cometary visitors; but we cannot, on the other hand, set aside the manifest lesson of literary history, the lesson that all great creative periods must end; that, viewing the whole course of thought, such periods are but few and far apart in the annals of mankind. And, however ingeniously theories of environment and ripeness for intellectual activity may explain the creative epochs of the past, no such theory is likely to receive formulation sufficiently precise to make it an accepted organon for the uses of forecast.

The creative period of German literature would have ended abruptly with the death of Goethe had not the genius of Heine given it fitful renewal of life for another quarter-century. In France, the modern creative period was clearly over when Hugo died. And in our own literature, it seems almost equally clear that the death of Tennyson has closed the Victorian age of letters, an age prolonged beyond the limits of most such periods of intellectual expansion, and one that, if our assumption be just, has 'made a good end.'

What may be expected to follow the period thus terminated? Whatever the literature to whose history we turn, we receive the same answer. After the creative age comes the age of reflection, the age of interpretation and analysis, of grammatical and rhetorical subtleties, of formulations and classifications, of scientific and imitative work. It was so with Greece and Rome, with fifteenth century Italy, with seventeenth century France and Spain, with post-Elizabethan England and post-Goethean Germany. That it will be so with the coming age, for France and the English-speaking nations, is a proposition at least as reasonable as many historical inductions that pass unquestioned.

But if we are passing into such an age we need not look upon it altogether with dismay. Those who live in such an age are far from conscious that theirs is a period of decadence. Intellectual activity seems to be heightened rather than depressed. Works of all sorts are produced and find no lack of readers. The Alexandrians thought the 'Argonautica' quite as good a poem as the 'Odyssey,' and the Florentines were doubtless perfectly sincere in their admiration of Poliziano. For those whom the *Zeitgeist* does not deceive, there remain for study and enjoyment the great works of the past, and there are enough of these for the lifelong contentment of any rational soul who finds his way to them. The art of criticism flourishes, but, although stiffened into a body of dogmatic precept, often enough goes hand in hand with genuine appreciation. It is not true that, properly to enjoy literature, an age must produce literature of its own. If the coming generation of English letters were to prove one of sterility, the wise should have slight cause for regret. It will be a long while before our race outgrows the ideals of Shelley and Wordsworth and Tennyson; some of them, it is to be hoped, neither our race, nor mankind, will ever outgrow. Indeed, the prospect of new masterpieces in uninterrupted succession would be rather appalling than otherwise. We should despair of catching up, and the works made classical by the infallible test of time would suffer more neglect than they do now. The real interests of culture almost demand such breathing-spells as, by a natural law no less beneficent than mysterious, follow upon the periods that have exhausted themselves in giving expression to the struggles of the spirit in its ascent from 'the sloughs of a low desire.' But the critical and reflective age has its dangers, and chief among them is the encouragement it gives to the ascendency of the cult.

The literary cult has two principal forms: it appears as the unintelligent (because unsympathetic) worship of a really great writer, or it takes the shape of laudation, both undue and uneven, of a writer of only secondary importance. In the first case, it converts the object of its adoration into a fetich, worshipping it as such rather than as a living spiritual force. In the second case, it raises a private altar for the exclusive use of the elect, and develops in its adherents a sort of intellectual priggishness, as satisfactory to them as it is amusing to others. A great deal of the modern study of Homer and Dante and Shakespeare illustrates the first form of the literary cult; the second form receives illustration at many hands, the devotees of Browning and Mr. Meredith, of Baudelaire and M. Verlaine, of Dr. Ibsen and Count Tolstoï, offering a few of the later examples.

We have said that the cult of such writers as these takes the shape of a laudation that is both undue and uneven. It is upon the second of these characteristics that stress should principally be laid, for the most astonishing feature of the Browning or the Baudelaire or the Ibsen cult is its deliberate neglect of the really great qualities of these men, and the emphasis given the accidental and inartistic aspects of their work. Nobler poetry than may be found in the work of Browning hardly occurs in English literature, but the work of the Browning societies would not often lead us to suspect its existence. Baudelaire touched with a master hand some of the deepest chords of human feeling, but those who magnify his name are apt to fix our attention upon the charnel-house elements of his verse, and almost make us sympathize with the recent suggestion of M. Brunetière, that the proposed statue of the poet should be placed at the mouth of a sewer. Dr. Ibsen, in his deeper moods, speaks with an ethical fervor that seems to his readers the very bread of life, but those who sing his praises in the public ear only ask us to admire the trivialities or the morbid features of his analysis of modern society. It is not surprising that a writer like Mr. Frederic Harrison, having, to begin with, but little sense of humor, should allow his indignation at such critical antics to get the better of amusement, and indulge in the following outburst:

'I know that, in the style of to-day, I ought hardly to venture to speak about poetry unless I am prepared to unfold the mysterious beauties of some unknown genius

Literature and Criticism

who has recently been unearthed by the Children of Light and Sweetness. I confess I have no such discovery to announce. I prefer to dwell in Gath and to pitch my tents in Ashdod; and I doubt the use of the sling as a weapon in modern war. I decline to go into hyperbolic eccentricities over unknown geniuses, and a single quality or power is not enough to rouse my enthusiasm. It is possible that no master ever painted a buttercup like this one, or the fringe of a robe like that one; that this poet has a unique subtlety, and that an undefinable music. I am still unconvinced, though the man who cannot see it, we are told, should at once retire to the place where there is wailing and gnashing of teeth.'

To the first form of the literary cult, the form which attaches itself to a really great name, our attention is called by a letter from Friedrich Spielhagen, on the Goethe-Schiller cult in Germany, published not long ago in the New York 'Nation.' The cult in question has been going merrily on for more than half a century, and Herr Spielhagen tells us, in substance, that it has been fruitful enough in science, but hardly at all in literature.

'I consider,' he says, 'as being two very different things, learned inquiries about the acts of a hero of genius, and the noble, broadening influence and effect of these actions on the life and blood, so to speak, of his country. The most painstaking and ingenious commentaries on the "Iliad" and "Odyssey" were indited at Alexandria, a whole library was filled with them, and yet Homer's sun set, and not all this flattering learned art could start it on its course again. I fear that much the same thing might be said of our Goethe-Schiller cult. The old text holds good here : "By their fruits ye shall know them." Where, I ask, are the fruits in our art and literature which have ripened in the Goethe-Schiller sun ? Where do we find in our poetry of to-day Goethe's delicate and sure feeling for the beautiful in form ? where his really living in the things which he describes ? where Schiller's flights of fancy which wafted him high above the mean and vulgar, "which enslaves us all "?'

The true cult of a great poet is very different from the form that is commonly practiced. When the day of that cult dawns, to quote once more from Herr Spielhagen, 'it will be understood that — always *mutatis mutandis* — one must do as Goethe and Schiller did. Till that day comes, let the disciples of Goethe and Schiller go on spreading wider and wider their silent influence. But, while they keep alive the sacred fire, let them have a care not to weaken their cause by crying, "Lord, Lord." For nothing is worse than publicly proclaiming one's self high-priest of the Father in Heaven and then sacrificing to Baal.' These words permit of a far wider application than their author gives them, for they indicate the eternal distinction between the true cult and the false in the domain of literature.

THE LITERARY WEST.

MR. LOWELL'S famous essay 'On a Certain Condescension in Foreigners' is in need of a supplement. 'A Certain Condescension in Easterners' is a theme that calls for treatment in similar vein ; but the pen rusts that alone could have dealt with it adequately, that alone could have bestowed upon it the measure and quality of genial satire that it deserves. For many years past the attitude of Eastern writers towards literary activity in the West has been similar to that once assumed by Boston towards New York, and by England towards the United States. It has been an attitude of condescension, of patronizing counsel, of mild surprise that a region so far removed from the centre of the intellectual system should venture to have such things as literary aspirations.

'But you are so very far away,' was the *naïve* remark recently made to a gathering of American scholars by a foreign guest who was trying to be complimentary, but who could not refrain from coupling surprise with admiration. Most Eastern explorers who brave the passes of the Alleghany Mountains, and find their way to the intellectual frontier settlements of the Mississippi Valley, return to their homes with a tale from which the element of wonder is rarely missing. Every now and then some weekly paper or monthly magazine of the Atlantic coast devotes an article to Western literature, and, whatever the aspect it selects for treatment or the writers it singles out for fame, the accent of encouragement is always marked.

This display of provincialism is amusing enough to all but the few who live in the intellectual corners where it originates; but it has one feature which has not been given the prominence that it deserves. As far as condescension goes, with its patronizing implications, the classical essay already mentioned may possibly be thought to cover the ground, for, *mutatis mutandis*, its criticism is applicable to New England narrowness as well as to Old England insularity. But the phase of the matter which seems to call for particular comment, and upon which Lowell hardly touched, is that illustrated by the kind of literary production which, in both cases, attracts the attention of the elder community to the work of the younger. Americans are not a little diverted when they notice the sort of thing upon which European critics of our literature are wont to seize as typical of our intellectual activity. 'Your countrymen,' says Richard Grant White, in the character of Mansfield Humphreys, speaking to his English fellow-traveller, 'even the intelligent and kindly-intentioned, are so stung with a craze after something peculiarly American from America that they refuse to accept anything as American that is not extravagant and grotesque. Even in literature they accept as American only that which is as strange and really as foreign to the tastes and habits of the most thoroughbred Americans as it is to them.' To this propensity of the European we must in large measure attribute the astonishing transatlantic vogue of Poe and Whitman and Mr. Harte. Excellent writers all three, and certainly among the foremost that this country has produced; yet it is to their accidental characteristics, rather than to their display of the qualities common to all good literature, that they in great part owe their reputation abroad. To quote once more from the writer above mentioned, the foreign critic is constantly putting to our literature such a question as this: 'Where is that effluence of the new-born individual soul that should emanate from a fresh and independant democracy, the possessors of a continent, with a Niagara and a Mississippi between two vast oceans?' And the foreign critic, finding this 'effluence of the new-born individual soul' to emanate very perceptibly from such a writer as Whitman, seizes upon him as a typically American product. To the sane student, of course, these characteristics of Whitman that so impress the foreigner are the husks of his genius; they are in themselves intolerable, but we put up with them because of the fitful flashes of imaginative style that find their way through these uncouth wrappings. But the foreigner takes the envelope for the substance; while for the American literature that is merely good, according to the accepted and immutable standards of literary workmanship, he has but scant recognition.

This peculiar attitude of the foreign critic toward American writers is closely paralleled by the attitude of the East toward the West; and this brings us to the special subject of our remarks. When an Eastern writer undertakes to discuss the literary activity of the West, he almost invariably falls into the error of the foreign critic, and singles out as noteworthy and typical the writers whose work evinces some sort of eccentricity. It may be badly written, it may be grotesque, it may be vulgar — it frequently has all three of these characteristics,— but it is original, it is piquant, it satisfies the unholy yearning for the new thing. Some composer of dialect doggerel, cheaply pathetic or sentimental, gains the ear of the public; his work has nothing more than novelty to recommend it, but the advent of a new poet is heralded, and we are told by Eastern critics that the literary West has at last found a voice. Some strong-lunged but untrained product of the prairies recounts the monotonous routine of life on the farm or in the country town, and is straightway hailed as the apostle of the newest and consequently the best realism. Some professional buffoon strikes a new note of bad taste in the columns of the local newspaper, and the admiring East holds him up as the exemplar of the coming humor. Some public lecturer, sure of the adulation of his little coterie of followers, estimates or interprets the literature of the world in accordance with whatever vagaries occupy his unregulated fancy, and the surprising announcement is made that a great creative critic has arisen in our midst. Skilled in the arts of self-advertisement, these men are quick to enlarge the foothold thus gained; their reputations grow like snowballs: they come to take themselves as seriously as they are taken by others; and the people of real culture and refinement, whose numbers are so rapidly increasing in the West, have to endure the humiliation of being represented, in the minds of a large proportion of their fellow-countrymen, by men who are neither cultured nor refined. In the meanwhile, hundreds of men and women throughtout the West are engaged in producing literary work too excellent to be obtrusive, work that conforms to the recognized standards of all serious writing, work that scorns to be effective at the cost of style and moderation and good taste. But if the average Eastern reader be asked who, in his mind, are the representative writers of the West, he will name persons indignantly repudiated, for the most part, by

Western readers of intelligence and discrimination. The selection will doubtless be made in good faith, and the fault will not be his; it will be the fault of the newspapers that have supplied him with the information, of the careless critics who make it a matter of faith that whatever is Western must needs be wild. A heavy responsibility rest with these critics both for the part they play in giving notoriety to scribblers who offend against art, and for their persistent failure to recognize the really praiseworthy work done by Western writers.

We do not claim that this work is as yet very great in amount, or that much of it deserves very high praise; but we do claim that it is respectable both in quality and quantity, and that both of these facts are to a considerable extent ignored by Eastern writers. We expect that the West will make a large contribution to American literature during the coming ten or twenty years; and, if ever sane criticism is needed, it is at such a time. But the criticism we get tends to discourage honest workmanship and to encourage what is extravagant and meretricious. Above all, it is time to have done with the notion, forced upon us with wearisome iteration by certain writers, both Eastern and Western, that the West is now developing, or ever will develope, a distinctive literature of its own. The West and the East are peopled by the same sort of men and women, and their work, when it deserves the name of literature at all, has, and will have, the characteristics common to all good writing in the English language. The distinction between East and West will never be other than an artificial one; even now, many of the best writers of either section came to it from the other. If the national centre of literary activity follows the Westward path of the centre of population, as seems probable, it will carry with it the accepted literary tradition, before which all crude local growths of tradition will be forced to give way. The coming literature of the West may be largely Western in its themes, but it will never be Western in its manner, as certain blatant rhetoricians would persuade us. Except in their relation to choice of subject-matter, the terms Eastern and Western, Northern and Southern, have absolutely no literary meaning in a country all of whose parts have a common speech. The same standards apply to all the literature written in the English language, whether produced in England or Australia, in Canada or the United States. Still more closely do they apply to the literature produced in different sections of our country, and it is an unfortunate application of local patriotism, whether Eastern or Western, that seeks to create a distinction where none should exist, or that, in its endeavor to create such a distinction, ignores the necessary unity of a national literature, and attaches undue weight to the accidental qualities of its particular manifestations.

THE WRITER AND HIS HIRE.

THE notion that literary work should not be done for pay, that it should be exempted from the commercial conditions under which man ordinarily does service to his fellows, is one that frequently finds expression (and sometimes most unexpectedly) among professional men of letters. It has more than once proved an obstacle in the path of the London Society of Authors, and has probably been among the causes that have thus far prevented an effective similar organization of the literary workers of our own country. Mr. Walter Besant has done yeoman service in combatting this idea among Englishmen, but it seems to have something of the hydra's vitality, and the severance of one head is but the signal for another to rear its crest. A recent deliverance upon this subject occurs in 'Scribner's Magazine,' and is of peculiar interest as expressing the opinion of a writer who is no less shrewd in the management of his business affairs than accomplished as a man of letters. Mr. Howells (for he it is to whom we refer) has a weakness for the paradoxical, and it is not always safe to take him quite as seriously as he reads. But his recent discussion of the literary life in its business aspect is prefaced by certain opinions which, allowing for an evidently whimsical element in their statement, still seem to embody the doctrine that it is ignoble to write for pay. Mr. Howells is, indeed, careful to say that, under existing conditions, a writer is bound to take pay for his work; but he vaguely intimates that existing conditions are all wrong, that there is something essentially degrading in a writer's acceptance of compensation for his work, and that in an ideal state of society the man of letters would somehow be taken care of without sharing in the contentions of the marketplace.

We are inclined to think that Mr. Howells has not gone far enough in his analysis of the problem. The man of letters is, like other men, whether Jew or Gentile, ' fed with the same food, hurt with the same weapons, subject to the same diseases, healed by the same means, warmed and cooled by the same winter and summer.' In a word, the man of letters lives, and must have the means of subsistence. Shall he live by his pen or shall he find other sources of revenue, and leave to his hours of leisure the cultivation of literature? Many men of letters, doubtless, have taken the latter course; much of the best literature has been produced under such conditions. The very best literature will get itself written under the most adverse form of these conditions. When, once in the centuries, a man has it in him to produce a 'Don Quixote' or a 'Divine Comedy,' he will follow the star that lights his soul to the accomplishment of its divine purpose. Mr. Howells thinks that Milton was overpaid for his 'Paradise Lost,' and doubtless he was, in the sense that the bookseller's paltry stipend did nothing to strengthen the motive that impelled to the composition of the epic. But we must remember that literature consists of more than the supreme masterpieces; that the minor masterpieces are serviceable in their way; and that the work of the honest journeyman is not without its uses. That the pursuit of literature should be relegated to the spare hours of men who earn their living otherwise, is a principle hardly to be defended, and Mr. Howells certainly does not mean to have us take that view. The application of such a principle would spare us many worthless books, no doubt; but it would also deprive us of much work, helpful in its generation, that we could ill do without.

But if, on the other hand, literature is a legitimate profession, an occupation to which it is well that many men should devote their best energies and their entire lives, there seems to be no good reason why it should not fit into the general scheme of society and share in the advantages of its economic organization. That organization may at present work in a way very unsatisfactory to the ethical sense, but not even Mr. Howells will deny it to be better than the barbarism which it has superseded, and to represent a necessary stage in the evolution of the civilized life. Mr. Howells seems to think that the ideal society of the future will somehow take charge of the literary artist and care for him as for a public benefactor, that it will provide him with maintenance in the Prytaneum. It is here, we think, that the analysis is defective. Under anything like the existing social organization, such public maintenance would merely shift the burden of the artist's support from his own special public to the public in general. He would still be paid for his work, having merely a new paymaster, probably less intelligent than the old one. But under the socialistic organization that Mr. Howells probably has in mind, we can see no reason why the artist should be singled out for special consideration. The honest ditch-digger is a public benefactor no less than the honest poet, and, if there be anything ignoble in the acceptance of pay for honest work, it is equally degrading to the manhood of both. All work, whether it be the digging of ditches or the writing of epics, is service done by man to his fellow-men. There are but two things that need concern the worker: let him take heed that the work be worth doing, and that it be serviceably performed. The real degradation, whether in literature or in any other form of activity, lies either in the doing of work that is essentially worthless, or in the doing of any kind of work for other than its own sake.

With the literary worker, the greater danger of degradation comes from the second of these causes. While we must admit the principle to be legitimate, the frank acceptance of literature as a commercial product, to be bought and paid for at the market rates, does result in attracting to the literary profession a large number of workers who have no higher aim than that of turning the profession of writing to the greatest possible pecuniary account. But the moral to be drawn from this state of things is precisely the same as that to be drawn from any other occupation. Work for the mere purpose of gain is always ignoble, no matter what sort of work it may be. Upon this point, Mr. Ruskin has given us the whole ethical doctrine, has interpreted the law and the prophets, in his lecture on 'Work.'

'It is physically impossible for a well-educated, intellectual, or brave man to make money the chief object of his thoughts; just as it is for him to make his dinner the principal object of them. All healthy people like their dinners, but their dinner is not the main object of their lives. So all healthy-minded people like making money — ought to like it, and to enjoy the sensation of winning it: but the main object of their life is not money; it is something better than money. A good soldier, for instance, mainly wishes to do his fighting well. He is glad of his pay — very properly so, and justly grumbles when you keep him ten years without it—still, his main notion of life is to win battles, not to be paid for winning them. So of clergymen. They like pew-rents, and baptismal fees, of course; but yet, if they are brave and well-educated, the pew-rent is not the sole object of their lives, and the baptismal fee is not the sole purpose of the baptism; the clergyman's object is essentially to baptize and preach, not to be paid for preaching. . . . And so with all other brave and rightly-trained men; their work is first, their fee second — very important always, but still second. But in every nation, as I said, there are a vast class who are ill-educated, cowardly, and more or less stupid. And with these people, just as certainly the fee is first, and the work second, as with brave people the work is first and the fee second.'

In a word, every man toiling with hand or head has the twofold ethical responsibility of choosing his work well and of doing it well. But in the special case of the literary toiler, the essence of doing well is to be sincere, truthful, and lofty of aim. If his work be done in this spirit, he need feel no shame in accepting, or even in stipulating for, its just reward, whether he be a journalist or a historian, a novelist or a poet. And if the time ever comes when all work is done in this spirit, we shall probably discover the existing social organization, based upon private contract and the utmost individual freedom, to be the real Utopia of which impatient idealists have been dreaming throughout the ages.

THE CRITIC AND HIS TASK.

'WE read far too many poor things,' said Goethe to Eckermann, 'thus losing time and gaining nothing.' In similar vein and at greater length, Schopenhauer gave vent to this characteristic outburst:

'The amount of time and paper — their own and other people's — wasted by the swarm of mediocre poets, and the injurious influence they exercise, are matters deserving of serious consideration. For the public is ever ready to seize upon novelty, and has a natural proneness for the perverse and the dull as most akin to itself. Therefore the works of mediocre poets divert public attention, keeping it away from the true masterpieces and the education they offer; acting in direct antagonism to the benign influence of genius, they ruin taste more and more, retarding the progress of the age. Such poets should therefore receive the scourge of criticism and satire without indulgence or sympathy, until led, for their own benefit, to apply their talents to reading what is good rather than to writing what is bad. For if the bungling of the incompetent so aroused the wrath of the gentle Apollo that he could flay Marsyas, I do not see upon what the mediocre poet can base his claim to tolerance.'

In such comment as we have just quoted there is a vein of bitterness not altogether to the taste of our complacent and easy-going modern age, so zealous in bearing witness to its democratic faith that it grudges recognition of any aristocracy at all, even of one as imprescriptible as that of genius. Live and let live, give every man his due and a little more, credit the intention rather than the performance, are some of the formulas in which the modern spirit of comfortable optimism finds expression. When literary production is the subject of criticism there are many motives at work in the interest of leniency or excessive generosity. Leaving entirely out of the question the unabashed puffery, regulated by counting-room conditions, that parades as criticism in so many of our newspapers; taking into serious account only the critical writing that is, as far as conscious purpose goes, honest in its intent; this work is still often weakened by influences too insidious in their action to be distinctly felt, yet giving it a tendency which, in view of the larger interests of the reading public, is undoubtedly pernicious. The critic deficient merely in knowledge heeds too closely the warning example of the early critics of Shelley and Keats, of Wordsworth and Tennyson, and casts his anchors to windward, hoping thereby to save his reputation from the scorn in which theirs stands pilloried. The critic whose defects are of the heart rather than of the intellect, who is too amenable to social influences or of too kindly a disposition to give the work under examination the character he knows it to possess, softens the outlines of truth (often quite unconsciously), and produces a distinctly false impression. In either case the public is served to its detriment rather than to its profit. The critic's paramount duty is, of course, his duty to the public, and every personal or private influence whatsoever must be resisted by him from the moment that its presence is felt.

All this is not easy, and yet it may be done by a writer who has both knowledge and honesty. If a book has little or no value, the fact must be clearly and firmly stated, no matter what the author under discussion may feel. This assignment to its place of a new book need not be done with the traditional brutality of the Quarterly reviewer, although even that would be better than the insipidity of the twaddle that so often passes for criticism, and that is obviously enough intended to win the good opinion of the author as well as so to hoodwink the public that its good opinion shall not be forfeited. How few critics there are who, recognizing the worthlessness of books, are yet ready, in Milton's phrase, to 'do sharpest justice on them as malefactors'? In fact, the sin of the Quarterly reviewers was not so much brutality as ignorance. Their attitude was hopelessly provincial, and they sought to conceal their limitations by the vigor of their invective. After all, a new book is bound to show an adequate reason for its being; if no such reason exists, the fact cannot be too soon discerned and stated. A new book is an attempt to divert the attention of readers from those already in their possession; it is an impertinence unless it bears a sufficient warrant. Books of knowledge must be multiplied with the advance of science, and their warrant is found in new facts and in the more perfect formulation of old ones. What Mr. Ruskin calls 'books of the hour' are warranted by the special interests of the hour. 'We ought to be entirely thankful for them, and entirely ashamed of ourselves if we make no good use of them.' With books of these classes, the task of the critic is simple. He must seize upon their elements of novelty or of timeliness, and must determine whether or not they accomplish their purpose.

With books that pretend to be additions to literature proper—with poems, plays, and novels—his task is different. He must be alert to detect new notes of song or of passion, but if only feeble echoes reward the search he must make the fact perfectly clear. Of the books of *belles-lettres* published during a given year, it is certainly safe to say that nine out of ten should never have seen the light, that in at least this fraction of the total number there is neither wit, nor invention, nor grace of style, nor harmony of numbers, in any redeeming measure. And the critic who persuades his readers that acquaintance with these empty books is more desirable than acquaintance with the recognized masterpieces — that it is desirable at all in view of the real literature waiting to be read — is careless of his responsibility and false to his trust.

There is, after all, but one standard in literature, and that is the highest. The great writers not only offer us boundless delight in themselves, but they provide us with a touchstone for the testing of all spurious metal. In a certain sense, it is the critic's business to make his readers independent of criticism, just as the physician's aim must be to make his patients independent of medicine. And the reader who has formed his taste upon good models does not need the critic's services except for occasional guidance. But the readers who need those services for instruction, in these days of insignificant or worthless books profusely multiplied, are still many; and the critic who sets up as absolute any merely relative standard of excellence, who describes the work of talent in terms only applicable to the work of genius, who praises the echo of noble literary work without clearly indicating its derivative character, who does not frequently renew his own strength by draughts from the fountainheads of literary inspiration,— the work of this critic can be the source of no real helpfulness, and can only expect to share the speedy oblivion awaiting the books that it seems for a moment to magnify into component parts of permanent literature.

TOUCHSTONES OF CRITICISM.

WE believe it was Emerson who once said that he was always glad to meet people who recognized the immeasurable superiority of Shakespeare over other poets. The feeling has doubtless been cherished by many a reader besides; for, after all, what test of the sane outlook upon life, the deep sympathy with its manifold phases, the discriminative faculty that knows the ring of the precious metal from the base not in literature alone, could be equal to this? To know the great poets, and to be sure that they are the great poets, not from mere passive acceptance of the traditional appraisement, but from reasoned and sincere conviction,— this is one of the most desirable of possessions; for it betokens a well-ordered imagination, a just balance of the intellectual and emotional elements of the inner life, a capacity for the highest of all possible artistic satisfactions. A clever simulation of this attitude is sometimes encountered, but it cannot long de-

Literature and Criticism 63

ceive the elect. It is sure to unmask itself in relations of anything like intimacy, to fall back upon pilfered formulas obviously hollow as far as the one who flaunts them is concerned, to be caught napping when some peculiarly vital point is at issue, to betray by some trick of intonation, or gesture, or facial expression, the insincerity of the pretended appreciation.

Yet even this pretence of comprehension is not always to be condemned. If it be made merely for the sake of conventionality, not much may be urged in its favor; but if it result from the humility of a judgment confident that the estimates reinforced by successive generations must somehow be right, from the conviction that failure to perceive all the beauty that a clearer vision has discerned must be attributable to one's own spiritual defect, and from the determination to assume the proper initial attitude and patiently wait for enlightenment to come, then it is hardly chargeable with hypocrisy, and merits sympathy rather than disdain. In such a case, we aver, at least, the attitude in question is more becoming, to say nothing of its being more hopeful, than that of the out-and-out Philistine, who raises his strident battle-cry to some such effect as this — ' I don't know anything about poetry, but I know what I like '—and then proceeds to descant upon the beauties of some scribbler who does not deserve serious consideration at all. This sort of outburst is familiar enough to everyone who unwisely speaks of literature in the presence of people who get their intellectual sustenance from the sensational periodical of monthly or daily publication, or from the paper-covered fiction of the newstand, and politeness usually forbids the only sort of reply that is adequate to the occasion. The advice needed by a person of this type is, in Mr. Frederic Harrison's phrase, that ' he should fall on his knees and pray for a cleanlier and quieter spirit,' but it must be left unspoken, and a smile of pity is the only permissible substitute.

Undoubtedly the best general evidence that one is possessed of the cleanly and quiet spirit to which Mr. Harrison so feelingly alludes is afforded by a real pleasure in the accepted masterpieces of literary art, or at least in a considerable number of them. The reader whose joy in Shakespeare and Dante, in Virgil and Tennyson, in Homer and Shelley, in Goethe and Cervantes, is genuine and perennial, is entitled to feel some confidence in his judgment of the moderns, as yet unclassified and unranked; to him, literature is no trackless forest, but a familiar well-travelled highway, provided with sign-posts and landmarks. The great names of literature are touchstones which teach us unerringly to know the good from the meretricious, even among the slightest productions of the hour. For it is a mistake to assume that because the major poet is so immeasurably removed from the minor poet each must be judged by the standards of his own class. The hopeless confusion of perspective that results from this assumption is only too familiar to readers of current criticism. How often do we find some insignificant poetaster of the day characterized in terms that would give us pause were they applied to one of the master-singers of the world. How many 'new poets' have been noisily heralded during the last twenty years, only to be consigned to forgetfulness a few months later. These critical extravagances are extremely unfortunate, for they bewilder the seeker after the beautiful, leading him into many a will-o'-the-wisp-haunted morass, besides tending to bring all criticism into disrepute. They are probably responsible in large measure for the amazing opinion, to which recent years have given considerable currency, that criticism has no business to be anything more than a subjective record of the critic's impressions, an unreasoned enumeration of his likes and dislikes.

But however prevalent such an opinion may become among the superficially-minded, genuine criticism, based upon the fundamental principles of art, is not likely to abdicate its function, any more than genuine economics is likely to abandon its scientific and rational procedure because of the subjective semi-emotional discussion that now in so many quarters usurps its name. And whatever the special method that criticism may choose to pursue, it will never forget that literary art exists, that its fundamentals have the sanction of the centuries, that any marked departure from those fundamentals is almost sure to be an indication of decadence or degeneracy, and that approved literature provides an almost infallible touchstone by which to test the value of the literature yet on trial. The best criticism is that which we get from those writers whose knowledge of the great poets is widest, and whose sense of their excellence is most unfailing. To narrow this suggested method from the general to the particular, we may say that Matthew Arnold's plan of keeping within memory's reach a few carefully selected examples of faultless diction, for purposes of comparison, is hardly to be improved upon. Arnold was entirely right in saying that to recognize the 'grand style' by this sort of touchstone we do not need to be able to define it, and he might have added that no kind of a definition would help anyone to recognize it who, when brought into its presence, could remain unconscious thereof. What he says of the 'grand style' is equally applicable to the other types of style which literature embodies. Symonds suggested a similar test of lyric excellence when he said that 'a genuine liking for "Prometheus Unbound" may be reckoned the touchstone of a man's capacity for understanding lyric poetry.' And as Arnold tells us that the reader who does not intuitively recognize the 'grand style' in Milton's 'Standing on earth, not rapt above the pole,' etc., can expect no other answer than 'the Gospel words: *Moriemini in peccatis vestris*,' so Symonds tells us that 'if a critic is so dull as to ask what " Light of Life ! thy lips enkindle " means, or to whom it is addressed, none can help him any more than one can help a man whose sense of hearing is too gross for the tenuity of a bat's cry.'

Perhaps a word may be said, in closing, of another sort of touchstone, one having no objective value to speak of, yet subjectively of considerable interest to many of us. There are several pretty tales going about of life-long friendships formed and cemented by a common love for FitzGerald's 'Omar.' Akin to these in their suggestion is the beautiful story of the Sicilians and their love for Euripides, the story which Browning has immortalized in the first adventure of Balaustion. Almost everyone who is widely read in literature takes to his heart of hearts some poet, as often as not of inferior rank, whose message is yet of such a nature as to make the strongest possible appeal to the individual idiosyncrasy. Such a poet becomes, to the one whose heart he has reached, a sort of touchstone to be applied to the rest of mankind, a test of the sympathies that must underlie real intimacy. But it should not be forgotten that this personal appeal to a few individuals here and there does not warrant them in reckoning their poet among the great singers of the world. We should not confuse the subjective standards of criticism with the objective ones, strong as is the temptation so to do. Even the sanest and most experienced critics do not always escape this confusion. Victor Hugo, for example, means a great deal to Mr. Swinburne personally, and so Mr. Swinburne, presumably writing what he intends for objective criticism, bestows deplorably extravagant praises upon the poet. On the other hand, Matthew Arnold, not liking some things about Shelley, is impelled to register the opinion that his prose is better than his poetry. It is hard to say which of these two vagaries is the more disheartening. If such men are capable of such lapses, what may we hope of lesser critics? One thing, at least, is clear. It cannot be asserted too frequently or too insistently that the likes or the dislikes of a critic have nothing to do with criticism, if the term is to be taken intelligibly. The argument, 'This work is good because I like it, and this other work is not good because I dislike it,' is nothing more than childish dogmatism, and quickly leads to some such *reductio ad absurdum* as has been illustrated. In any objective sense, no merely personal preference, however strongly felt, is to be reckoned among the touchstones of genuine criticism.

ANONYMITY IN LITERARY CRITICISM.

THE question of responsibility for criticism is one of the most difficult with which the literary profession has to deal. Should it be signed or unsigned, personal or impersonal; should it express the opinion of an individual or of an organ? The question has been ably and amply discussed from both points of view, and both systems (in English-speaking countries, at least) have been found to work well in practice. In behalf of the principle of anonymity it is argued, first, that criticism has increased weight when put forth with all the authority of a paper or review that has gained the confidence of the public; second, that by this method alone is untrammelled criticism, free from personal obligations or reservations, to be secured. Upon these two leading arguments the case for anonymity rests; others are occasionally brought forward, but examination shows them to be either of a derivative nature or of minor importance.

In behalf of the criticism for which personal responsibility is assumed, we are told, first, that all such criticism really *is* the work of individuals, and that it is unworthy to pretend that it is anything else; second, that intentional unfairness is less likely to be displayed when authorship is avowed than when it is concealed; third, that injustice is done to the critic himself when the periodical to which he contributes assumes all the credit for his work, and that this assumption reacts upon the work, tending to make it colorless and weak.

It is hardly necessary for us to say, in so many words, that the arguments for personal responsibility seem to us the weightier, since we have, from the start, adhered to the practice of publishing signed criticisms of all the important works reviewed in 'The Dial.' While granting that the impersonal system has some advantages, it seems to admit of still more abuses. The nature of these abuses has been succinctly set forth by Mr. Besant in a recent article. He says:

'I should rejoice to see the custom of signing criticisms in literature and art become general, for several reasons. First, because it would instantly, I believe, de-

Literature and Criticism

molish the flippant smartness and insolence with which some papers allow their columns to be disfigured—smartness which disguises the fact that the critic knows nothing of his subject; it would force the writer at least to read the book; it would put an end to the reviewing of books in the batch; it would make the young critic anxious to advance his own name as a writer who can deliver carefully considered judgment in the courteous language of a gentleman; this language he would study to preserve in his work, or to learn if he had never learned it; and it would enormously raise the position and status of a critic in the eyes of the editor, as well as those of the reading public. That it would also rapidly advance the capable critic in his own profession may be taken for granted.'

For these reasons, and for others of a similar character, we think it desirable that the authorship of literary criticism should, as a rule, be acknowledged.

There is, however, one abuse connected with the system of signed reviews that requires a moment's consideration. When this system is in use, the temptation is strong to secure the names of well-known writers, regardless of their fitness for the work. We have far too much of this misdirected effort, both in the sensational press of the day and of the month. Some periodicals of the sort in question even display title-pages or tables of contents in which the names of their contributors appear in heavy-faced type, while the subjects of the contributions are printed in the most modest and inconspicuous of characters. In fact, one of the greatest vices of our periodical press is this willingness to appeal to the public ear by means of names rather than by means of serious and competent discussion. When the subject considered is subordinated to the personality of the man who writes about it, we have reached something very like a *reductio ad absurdum* of the system. At all events, we have shown how a system, excellent in principle, may be condemned by its own excesses. On the other hand, the anonymous system too easily lends itself to concealment of the poverty of the resources at the command of a review. When criticism is to be unsigned, there is an increased difficulty in obtaining criticism of the best quality, and editors will sometimes succumb to the temptation afforded by the fact that, however inefficient the work offered them may be, it must share in the general prestige of the periodical in which it appears. As regards the two abuses just considered, the one appears to be no more probable or dangerous than the other; in either case, the abuse in question will not be chargeable to any editor who accepts the responsibility of his position. In other words, the editor who is determined to present his readers with serious and honest criticism will refuse to publish incompetent work, whether it come baited with a well-known name or bear no name at all.

When we consider the influence upon the writer himself (assuming him to be competent) of the knowledge that his work is to be signed or unsigned, it seems to us that the argument for personally acknowledged criticism is much the better. It is so easy for the anonymous critic to be unfair, to allow his work to be colored by a personal prejudice against which it is impossible for the reader to be on his guard. The best of the anonymous reviews show occasional examples of very uncritical prejudice, which, as a rule obvious enough to the expert in such matters, is entirely unperceived by the average reader. Sometimes, indeed, the prejudice is so deftly concealed as to impose upon the very elect. That this evil is greatly lessened when criticism is acknowledged should be apparent enough. There are cases, no doubt, in which the reviewer who is to sign his criticism will fail, for personal reasons, to speak out his whole mind, and an occasional work may, in consequence, receive a more generous measure of praise than it deserves. But this evil appears to us of minor importance when compared with the evil of prejudice protected by anonymity, and unrestrained by any sense of personal responsibility. Without going as far as Schopenhauer, when he calls anonymity the 'shield of all literary rascality,' we may find a certain satisfaction in his vigorous denunciation of the system.

'It was introduced under the pretext of protecting the honest critic, who warned the public against the resentment of the author and his friends. But where there is one case of this sort there will be a hundred where it merely serves to take all responsibility from the man who cannot stand by what he has said, or possibly to conceal the shame of one who has been cowardly and base enough to recommend a book to the public for the purpose of putting money into his own pocket. Often enough it is only a cloak for covering the obscurity, incompetence, and insignificance of the critic. It is incredible what impudence these fellows will show, and what literary trickery they will venture to commit, as soon as they know they are safe under the shadow of anonymity.'

There is much force in this, and there is pith in the author's further suggestion that a man should be answerable for what he writes, 'at any rate with his honor, if he has any; and if he has none, let his name neutralize the effect of his words.'

Thus we see that one of the two leading arguments for anonymity does not seem, upon careful examination, to be well based. The other argument — that criticism bearing the authority of a review has greater weight than that which bears but the authority of an individual — might be dismissed with the question: Why should criticism have any greater weight than attaches to the authority of its writer? But there is really more than this to be said upon the subject. A critical periodical should be more than a mere collection of essays. It is a pitiful theory that regards a review as a mere dumping-ground for all sorts of opinions. A review should stand for something; it should represent sane intelligence upon the subjects with which it is concerned; it should march in the vanguard of thought. M. Zola, who has recently, in his address before the London Conference of Journalists, stirred up the question of anonymity, goes astray at this point. His plea is for personal responsibility in criticism, and is excellently urged, but he attempts to make an unreal distinction between political and literary criticism. He expresses the opinion that political discussion should be impersonal, and adds:

'At the same time I confess that if I recognize the necessity for anonymity in political matters, I am none the less surprised that it can exist in literary matters. Here I entirely fail to grasp the situation. I refer especially to articles of criticism, judgments pronounced upon the play, the book, the work of art. Can there be such a thing as the literature, the art of a party? That discipline, average opinion, should prevail in politics is certainly wise. But that a literary or artistic production should be adapted to suit the views of a whole party, that a scythe should be used to cut down everybody to the same level, that all should be mixed up in a common herd, in order to politely please your public, this I consider to be dangerous to the intellectual vitality of a nation. This sort of regimental criticism, speaking in the name of a majority, can only end in producing a mediocre, colorless literature.'

The mistake here is in the assumption that impersonal discussion, whether political or artistic, must be partisan. But it cannot for a moment be admitted that either the one or the other is necessarily partisan, except in the sense that it must take the part of knowledge against ignorance, of intelligence against dulness, of sanity against eccentricity, of rationality against irrationality. We do not decide against anonymous literary criticism because of its assumed tendency to become partisan, or to express average opinion—it cannot well be the one, and ought not to do the other—but for the far more cogent reasons above set forth and also recognized by M. Zola elsewhere in his address. It must be remembered that a critical review has to deal with all sorts of subjects, not only with *belles lettres*, but with history and science and philosophy as well. The word partisanship has no meaning when applied to so wide a range of interests.

Recurring once more to the main argument for anonymity, we would say, finally, that the criticism which is published in a review of high character and recognized authority does receive added weight from that very fact, if signed no less than if unsigned. We do not believe that the addition of a signature detracts from the authority of the criticism, and we are sure that it adds to the reader's confidence in the sincerity of the writer. If the name of the writer is well known, his opinion comes with the added authority of the review in which it appears; if the name is not well known, the importance to be attached to the opinion will be measured, not by the obscurity of the writer, but by the confidence which the editorial conduct of the review inspires. In a word, when critical articles are signed, there is at least no loss of weight, and there may be a distinct increment of gain. The last editions of the 'Encyclopædia Britannica' and of 'Chambers's Encyclopædia' are the better and the more authoritative from the fact that their chief contributions are acknowledged. 'The Fortnightly Review,' with its signed articles, quickly gained a higher prestige than had been enjoyed by the anonymous quarterlies. If 'The Athenæum' and 'The Saturday Review' and 'The Nation,' following the example of 'The Academy' and 'The Dial,' were to adopt the system of signed criticisms, they would probably exert a deeper influence than they do at present, and would certainly command a more unreserved confidence from their constituency.

POETRY AS CRITICISM OF LITERATURE.

We have heard much (something too much indeed) of poetry as a criticism of life, since the time when Matthew Arnold, in his essay on Wordsworth, started that famous phrase on its career. Its inadequacy has been pointed out by many critics since, and it is now, we should say, definitely relegated to the limbo of half-truths that fascinate for a time by virtue of their novelty, but that speedily become discredited. Probably the most convincing of the many protests it evoked was that of the writer who urged that, so far from being a mere criticism upon life, the greatest poetry is life itself, in direct transcription. But, while we must regard as whimsical the notion that poetry is nothing more than criticism, even glorified criticism, we may freely admit that there is to be found in poetical literature a large element critical of life and of many other things as well. Among those other things, literature itself is of considerable importance; and we here wish to say a few words about the treasures of literary criticism that are among the precious gifts brought us by the poet.

In this age of the multiplication of anthologies, it has for many years been to us a matter of surprise that someone did not prepare a volume of 'Poems of Poets,' to go with the 'Poems of Places,' the 'Poems of Books,' the 'Poems of Nature,' and the many other special collections. Within the last year or so, the want has been supplied, after a fashion, by two independent collections; and the lover of poets, as well as the owner of dogs and the smoker of tobacco, is now provided with his own anthology of favorite pieces. There is still room for a better collection than has yet been made, but the needs of a deserving class of readers have at least received recognition.

It has often been urged that the critic of any art should be at the same time an adept in the practice thereof. This view doubtless rests upon a misconception, being analogous to the view that no one can intelligently read a foreign language without speaking it as well. In the case of the language, as is sufficiently obvious, the process by which one acquires its use for reading is essentially unlike the process by which one learns to speak it. To speak psychologically, the nexus of associative tracks worn by much reading of French or Latin is one thing, and the nexus worn by much speaking of a foreign tongue quite another. To be more exact, we should perhaps say that the associative stimulus, while going over the same nerve-track in any particular case, takes one direction in the case of reading, and the reverse direction in the case of speech. Because the passage from word-symbol to concept is easily made, it by no means follows that the passage from concept to word-symbol will present no difficulty. A similar situation, although a far more complicated one, is presented when we compare the practice of literary composition with its criticism. But it is nevertheless true that the reader of a foreign tongue is better prepared to get its full significance if his associations have been trained to work freely in both directions; and it is likewise true that the critic of literature who has made literature himself is, *ipso facto*, in some respects better equipped to understand just what has been accomplished by his fellow workers. Only we must not go so far as to say that creative power brings with it the critical faculty; the former may indeed add something to the effectiveness of the latter, but the intuitional character of the one is still permanently differentiated from the reflective character of the other.

That the poets are capable of writing good prose criticism of their art, it needs no argument to show. We think at once of Lessing and Goethe, of Voltaire and Hugo, of Shelley and Coleridge, and of fifty others. We are now concerned to call attention to the fact that some of the most acute and sympathetic criticism of the poets that we have is to be found in poetry itself. Since English literature best illustrates this fact, although other literatures might profitably be adduced in further support of it, we shall be content with English examples alone. The good work of poetical criticism was begun by Chaucer, who labored under the disadvantage of having no fellow-poets of his own speech to sing about, and who was thus compelled to find subjects for his 'House of Fame' and other critical ventures in the great names of classical antiquity or of contemporary Italy. From Chaucer's time to the present, the work has gone merrily on, and the last of our great poets has written more good poetry about his fellow-singers than we owe to any of his predecessors.

The contemporaries and immediate followers of Chaucer had at least one English poet to panegyrize; and so Gower, and Occleve, and Lydgate, to the best of their mean powers, paid tribute to their master. Even to-day, do we not feel some thrill of sympathy when we read Occleve?

'O maister dere and fader reverent,
My maister Chaucer, flowre of eloquence,
Mirrour of fructuous entendement
O universal fader in science,
Allas! that thou thyne excellent prudence
In thy bedde mortel myghtest not bequethe
What eyled dethe, allas! why wolde he sle thee?'

When we come down to the Elizabethans, we find the poets rioting in versified criticism of one another. Shakespeare is a notable exception to this rule, and in the one case in which he displayed enthusiasm for a contemporary, and spoke of 'the proud full sail of his great verse,' he forgot to tell us whom he meant. There is a good deal of log-rolling, and no little malice, in all this personal poetry (such things have been known in later times, even in our own), but many of these tributes strike a note of sincerity, and display an insight for which we must ever cherish them. How true, for example, is Drayton's familiar description of Marlowe : 'His raptures were all air and fire'; and Barnfield's of Spenser: 'Whose deep conceit is such, as passing all conceit, needs no defense'; and Jonson's of Shakespeare: 'He was not for an age but for all time.'

It is curious to note, as we work down the centuries, how the taste of each age is reflected in these appreciations of poets by poets. In the seventeenth century, Milton and Dryden, indeed, as we might naturally expect of the two greatest men of their age, showed an understanding of Shakespeare's supremacy that leaves nothing to be desired; but the lesser men of the time clearly preferred the lesser Elizabethans, or the decadent artificers among their own contemporaries. The poets of our so-called Augustan age usually referred to the great English classics in a perfunctory sort of way, and gave them but a grudging recognition. It is very amusing to find Addi-

Literature and Criticism

son, with all the airs of the Superior Person, saying of Chaucer that 'In vain he jests in his unpolished strain,' and of Spenser, that he 'In ancient tales amused a barbarous age,' writing on the other hand of 'Great Cowley then, a mighty genius,' and going into rhapsodies over that 'harmonious bard,' the 'courtly Waller.' Equally amusing contrasted citations might be made from Pope. It was only in the later eighteenth century, with Collins and Gray, that poetry acquired a saner outlook upon itself, and began to grope back toward the old truth that art is better than artifice.

The nineteenth century is so rich in the homage of poet to fellow-poet, that an essay, rather than a paragraph, would be needed to do it justice. Wordsworth's sonnet to Milton, Shelley's 'Adonaïs,' Keats's 'Chapman's Homer,' Landor's sonnet 'To Robert Browning,' Mrs. Browning's 'Wine of Cyprus,' Rossetti's 'Dante at Verona,' Arnold's 'Thyrsis,' Tennyson's 'Alcaics,' and Mr. Swinburne's sonnets on the Elizabethan dramatists, are a few of the countless examples that will occur to every reader. And we would call particular attention to the fine critical quality of the mass of work which these poems so imperfectly represent. Their writers have good reasons for the faith that is in them; they do not merely eulogize, they illuminate as well. If this were not so, the present article would have no excuse for existence. We do not know where in prose to find better criticism than Wordsworth's of Milton:

> 'Thou hadst a voice whose sound was like the sea;
> Pure as the naked heavens, majestic, free,'

or Landor's of Browning:

> 'Since Chaucer was alive and hale
> No man has walk'd along our roads with step
> So active, so inquiring eye, or tongue
> So varied in discourse,'

or Arnold's of Goethe:

> 'He took the suffering human race,
> He read each wound, each weakness clear;
> And struck his finger on the place,
> And said: "Thou ailest here, and here!"'

or Mr. Swinburne's of Dante mourning over a country recreant to its mission and dead in spirit:

> 'The steepness of strange stairs had tired his feet,
> And his lips yet seemed sick of that salt bread
> Wherewith the lips of banishment are fed;

> But nothing was there in the world so sweet
>   As the most bitter love, like God's own grace,
>   Wherewith he gazed on that fair buried face.'

We hope that someone will undertake the preparation of an enchiridion of poetical criticism more comprehensive than has yet been attempted, a collection of the best things that have been said in the poetry of half a dozen modern literatures about the best poets of the whole world. Such a collection would be of the greatest value to the student of literary criticism, and would deserve to stand on the shelf beside the 'Poetics' of Aristotle, the treatise of Longinus, the impassioned pleas of Sidney and Shelley, and the essays of Coleridge, Arnold, and Pater.

THE NEGLECTED ART OF TRANSLATION.

These closing years of the nineteenth century have made us more cosmopolitan, in many respects, than we ever were before. The world has shrunk for us in several ways; as a mere matter of geography, the greater part of it is within easy reach; politically and socially, the sense of human solidarity is growing all the time; and in intellectual affairs it is safe to say that no voice having a real message to deliver is likely to wait long for appreciative listeners. Neglected genius seems to have become a thing of the past, and we now suffer instead from a tendency to exalt with undue precipitancy to the ranks of genius every questionable and imperfectly realized talent that appears upon the intellectual horizon. In literature particularly, we are alert as never before to catch the new note, to seize upon and exploit the new thing. Let a poet, or novelist, or essayist but raise his head in any corner of civilization, and, if his message be not purely provincial in its application, he will soon find himself translated into the tongues of the aliens, and his thoughts will find lodgment upon their lips. Nay, if the message be but a provincial one after all, it is not unlikely to incur the same fate, such has become our curiosity concerning all our fellow-men, such our insatiable demand for the new type and the local coloring.

This linking together of the literatures by translation is particularly noticeable among the peoples using the German, English, and French languages, and, as an intellectual tendency, has followed the order just named. Germany was the leader in the movement, and throughout most of the century, has been seizing with omnivorous appetite upon whatever was most notable in the literary product of other countries. Not only has she assimilated the productions of such peoples as the Hungarians, the Scandinavians, and the Slavs—peoples closely associated with her either politically or ethnically—but also those of the English and French, the Italian and Spanish. The works of Jókai, Œhlenschläger, and Pushkin first found a large foreign audience among the Teutons; Dante, Calderon, and Voltaire early became theirs by right of conquest, and the Shakespearian permeation of German literature is so familiar a fact as hardly to need mention. The English people, on either side of the Atlantic, have followed the Germans, although at a distance, in thus welcoming the foreigner to their hearth, and we all know the good work of Carlyle and Coleridge, in the English case, and of the Concord group of plain livers and high thinkers, in our own. France, maintaining longer than Germany or England her self-sufficient attitude, has more recently fallen into line, and the most desperate efforts of chauvinism have failed to protect her frontiers from the invasion of the alien writer. Indeed, the proposition that new converts are the most zealous of all, is well illustrated by the eager enthusiasm with which the Frenchman is nowadays taking up the foreigner and his works. The distinction is very marked, for example, between the polite curiosity with which Ampère explored Scandinavian literature for the information of Frenchmen half a century ago, and the genuine interest which is taken by Frenchmen of to-day in the works of the great Norwegians.

In our own country, while cordial recognition of the established names of foreign literature has not been lacking since mid-century, we have, until very recently, been slow to seize upon the work of new writers. Tourguénieff, for example, had long been naturalized in France and Germany before he was discovered by America. Dr. Ibsen had done the greatest and most enduring part of his work twenty years ago, but the voice of the student here and there among us who had discovered him was that of one crying in the wilderness. A few contemporary Germans and Frenchmen, somewhat capriciously selected, were known to our readers; others, equally important, were not known at all. As for the contemporary Italian, or Spaniard, or Pole, or Russian, his name was, with hardly an exception, meaningless to us. Most of us who studied the history of foreign literatures were content to stop with the dawn of the century; of active modern tendencies in the world of foreign letters we had not the least notion.

The rapidity with which, of late, *nous avons changé tout cela*, is a little surprising. The past few years have brought before our eyes, in bewildering succession, an array of contemporary writers from all parts of the civilized world. Novelists and dramatists, essayists and poets, of the most diverse nationalities and ideals, compete for our attention. Not only do the new works of the older literatures crowd upon us, but the new literatures of Canada, Australia, Greece, Portugal, and Spanish America as well. Now most of these new claimants for attention require conversion into our vernacular before we may become acquainted with them. And this fact leads us to the real consideration of the present article, which is, briefly, that the art of translation, so far from keeping pace with its practice, lags painfully behind. The more translations we get, the worse they seem to be. Time was when a translation was at least apt to be a labor of love, conscientiously and sympathetically performed. At present, it seems a sort of scramble to be first in the field. A novel by a popular foreign author is almost sure to get before our public in a translation so wooden, so unidiomatic, so essentially ignorant, as to be a mere travesty of the original. One who has occasion to examine many of these productions is only too often reminded of the sort of translation that was suffered by Bottom, and is surprised beyond measure when he comes upon a version which is not an utter perversion. We do not here speak of the ethical question, so often ignored by those who deliberately alter or curtail the text of their originals, but merely of the lack of intelligence and capacity nearly always displayed by translators of contemporary literature.

The simple fact is that the qualifications of a translator are set far too low, both by his employer and the public. The long-suffering public, of course, has to take what it can get, is too apathetic to demand better workmanship, and easily grows accustomed to the hack-work that dulls the taste and deadens the literary sensibility. As for the employer, the publisher, he finds a ready sale for the cheap product, and hence does not offer the compensation that good work ought to bring. Of course he has a moral responsibility in the matter, but he is not likely to care for that when his pocket is concerned. Any young person with a smattering of French or German and a dictionary to help him out, feels competent to become a translator, it never occurring to him that the cultivation of an English style is the first requisite of all; while the average publisher shows that he accepts this view by refusing to pay for translations any sum that a competent workman, the real master of two languages, can possibly accept. Of course, honorable exceptions to this rule may be found here and there, and equally of course good translations will now and then come from persons actuated, not by self-interest, but by a delight in good workmanship for its own sake. But the conditions that fix the existing standard of translation are still mainly of the hard commercial kind, and, until they are in some way modified, the standard will remain low.

It is possible that the art of translation may rise from its present disrepute, but the process will be slow. Cause for hopefulness may be found in two facts. The first of these facts is that the Copyright Act of 1891 for the first time gave the foreign writer some measure of control over the American publication of translations of his work. He has it in his power to secure an adequate translation, and to preëmpt the market for it. Unfortunately, he does not always know a good translation from a bad one, and even if he does, may find it difficult to arrange for what he wants. Possibly he may come to learn by experience how immeasurably his reputation suffers from blundering translations, and take measures to secure himself against them. The other cause for hopefulness is in the fact that an immense expansion has taken place of late years in the modern language departments of our educational institutions. The languages of Europe are pursued in the scientific and literary spirit by an increasing number of students every year. These students will make most of the translations that will be read by the coming decades. It is not too much to believe that their better methods and fuller knowledge will make itself felt more and more as the years pass, and that their efforts may cause a marked elevation in the current standard of literary translation.

EDUCATION

THE HIGHER AIM.

> Oh beati que' pochi che seggono a quella mensa ove il pane degli Angeli si mangia. — *Convito*, I., *1*.
>
> Pan degli Angeli, del quale
> Vivese qui, ma non sen vien satollo.
> — *Paradiso*, II., *11, 12*.

WE build and build; each generation's rise
    Brings us the old new question: what the way
    To shape the soul, and fit it for the fray
That is the life of man. Shall these suffice —
The rule of thumb, the formula concise,
    The pedant's wisdom hoarded day by day?
    Dry husks of fact — do these the toil repay?
Shall this of all our labor be the price?

Nay, truth our aim, and truth is more than fact;
Ere knowledge ripen into worthy act
    The spirit's glow must make it truth indeed,
Of ardent aspiration all compact,
    Such truth as Dante won in sorest need,
'Angelic bread' whereon the soul may feed.

A FEW WORDS ABOUT EDUCATION.

AT no previous time in the history of this country has the discussion of educational questions been so serious a preoccupation as it is at present. During the past quarter of a century we have become pretty thoroughly awakened, not so much to the importance of education, which has never been questioned, as to the importance of establishing education upon the right foundation, and of conducting it in accordance with the most enlightened methods. So great a fermentation in so important a department of thought is, of course, a desirable thing, even if its blessings be not wholly unmixed. It is well occasionally to shake off our torpor, to get out of ruts, to avoid stagnation at almost any cost. But such a condition of intellectual unrest, such a determination to reëxamine the old grounds of the faith, is always fraught with the danger that we may, in our haste to make all things new, sweep away the good with the bad, and discard some of the fundamental principles of the philosophy of a sound education.

Many zealous advocates of what they are pleased to call 'the new education' are so thoroughgoing in their notions that the temperate onlooker is compelled to view their proposed policy somewhat askance. They would have us believe that the world has hitherto been all astray, that the educational wisdom of the ages is little better than foolishness, that we are upon the eve of a reform in our practice which is to be nothing less than revolutionary in its effect. These theorists complain, briefly, that education has in the past been made too much a matter of words; the remedy they offer is to make it in the future chiefly a matter of things. To bring about this radical change it is proposed to displace to a great extent the sterile practices of literary, philological, and historical study by the productive practices with which physical science acquaints us, to substitute for the study of man in his social and political character the study of man in his character as a tool-making and tool-using animal, mainly intent upon material comfort and progress. The educational tendency here suggested is very marked at the present day, and the signs of the times in many ways force it upon our attention. It is a tendency more marked, perhaps, during recent years, than ever before, and more marked, probably, in our own country than in any other. This is a fact easily to be accounted for. The development of physical science is the dominant intellectual characteristic of the age, and this development, with its countless implied possibilities of material amelioration, has diverted many eyes from those things of the spirit that are so essential to the higher welfare of mankind, fixing them instead upon the objects which their lower natures demand; it has, in a word, substituted ideals of comfort for ideals of virtue and of the full-statured life of the soul. And this diversion of attention from the higher to the lower aims of life, this substitution of lesser ideals for greater, of ignoble for noble purposes, has been nowhere else so nearly complete as in this country of unexampled material resources and unexampled material prosperity.

Matthew Arnold, in one of his essays on religious subjects, has a passage exactly descriptive of our too prevalent attitude toward the educational problem. This passage, with the necessary substitution of 'the humanities,' or some such phrase, for the word 'religion,' runs as follows:

'Undoubtedly there are times when a reaction sets in, when an interest in the processes of productive industry, in physical science and the practical arts, is called *an interest in things*, and an interest in [the humanities] is called *an interest in words*. People really do seem to imagine that in seeing and learning how buttons are made, or *papier mâché*, they shall find some new and untried vital resource; that our prospects from this sort of study have something peculiarly hopeful and animating about them; and that the positive and practical thing to do is to give up [the humanities] and turn to them.'

Now a great many sincere and well-meaning people have been telling us of late that 'the positive and practical thing to do' in education is to set aside such useless studies as 'mere' history and literature, as 'dead' languages and ancient civilizations; to restrict considerably the attention paid to most other kinds of 'book' learning; and to devote the time thus reclaimed from waste to such scientific and even manual pursuits as are likely to have some direct bearing upon the everyday life of the men and women that our schoolchildren are so soon to become.

Education

Half-truths are often more dangerous than downright errors, and the consequences of the sciolist theory of education just outlined are in many directions manifest. For one thing, there is the loud outcry, heard in many quarters, for the introduction of 'manual training' into our common-school systems, not as an adjunct to intellectual training, which it may very properly become, but as a substitute for what is contemptuously styled the *Wortkram* of the old-fashioned systems. One persistent advocate of this particular nostrum goes so far as to say that in the ideal school of his imagining 'the highest text-books are tools, and how to use them most intelligently is the highest test of scholarship.' In the field of higher education, the same spirit is illustrated by the immense expansion of the technological and scientific departments of our universities, at the expense, too often, of the humanities, and by the determined warfare that has been waged, during the past score of years, upon the classical and other branches of the older education. Almost everywhere, too, the newspaper press has joined in the clamorous demand for a more 'practical' education; that is, for an education by whose aid the body may be fattened, however the soul be starved.

In the development of the current popular opinion upon this all-important subject, we may distinguish two phases. To begin with, science, in the first flush of its great mid-century achievements, put forth the arrogant plea that it alone was deserving of serious consideration as an educational discipline. Mr. Spencer's famous tractate upon 'Education' seemed to give cogency to this plea, and for a time did duty as a sort of gospel of the new dispensation. But the narrowness and inadequacy of that gospel became, after a while, apparent even to the less reflective of minds, and a new doctrine emerged to fit the altered educational attitude. That doctrine, which has lately been urged with considerable eloquence, is, substantially, that all subjects are equally valuable as intellectual disciplines, and that physics and biology, if pursued in the proper spirit, are as potent to build up the full-statured life as are history, and literature, and philosophy. But there are now indications that a third phase of the discussion is at hand, and that the question of relative educational values is about to receive a more searching examination than it has ever had before. And, in this connection, it is indeed significant that the President for 1895 of the National Educational Association, in preparing his inaugural address, should have felt that the time was ripe to use such words as the following:

'If it be true that Spirit and Reason rule the universe, then the highest and most enduring knowledge is of the things of the Spirit. That subtle sense of the beautiful and the sublime which accompanies spiritual insight, and is part of it, is the highest achievement of which humanity is capable. . . . The study of nature is entitled to recognition on grounds similar to those put forward for the study of literature, of art, and of history. But among themselves these divisions of knowledge fall into an order of excellence as educational material that is determined by their respective relations to the development of the reflective Reason. The application of this test must inevitably lead us, while honoring science and insisting upon its study, to place above it the study of history, of literature, of art, and of institutional life.'

Contrasted with such an ideal as this of the well-ordered education, how poor are all ideals that but proclaim the watchword of a narrow practicality. One of the finest expressions ever given to the nobler view is embodied in this passage from Newman's 'Idea of a University':

'That perfection of the Intellect, which is the result of Education, and its *beau idéal*, to be imparted to individuals in their respective measures, is the clear, calm, accurate vision and comprehension of all things as far as the finite mind can embrace them, each in its place, and with its own characteristics upon it. It is almost prophetic from its knowledge of history; it is almost heart-searching from its knowledge of human nature; it has almost supernatural charity from its freedom from littleness and prejudice; it has almost the repose of faith, because nothing can startle it; it has almost the beauty and harmony of heavenly contemplation, so intimate is it with the eternal order of things and the music of the spheres.'

Nor does this higher aim concern the advanced stages of educational work alone. It should be an inspiring force in the kindergarten no less than in the college, for the child, as well as the man, does not live by bread alone, unless, indeed, it be that 'pan degli Angeli' whereof Dante tells us. 'Those few,' he says, 'are blessed who sit at the board' where it is eaten. Let it be our task to make the few the many, and the largess such as knows no stint.

THE APPROACH TO LITERATURE.

An excellent educational method, much in vogue among the more progressive of modern teachers, is based upon the principle of proceeding from the near and the familiar to the strange and the remote. It is a method that may be pushed to extremes, but it is fundamentally sound. In geography, for example, a child starts with the schoolhouse, the village, and the surrounding country made familiar by his wanderings, and afterwards extends to scenes unvisited the construction thus begun. In history, the happenings of the day, as narrated in the newspapers and talked about by his acquaintances, provide the starting-point. In seeking to arrive at a comprehension of the nature and workings of government and the organization of society, his attention is first directed toward the town-meeting, which he has possibly seen at work; toward the policeman or the constable, whom he has learned to recognize as the embodiment of executive authority before having learned the meaning of that term; or toward the tax-collector, about whose visits certain ominous associations have clustered, before the function of that *persona non grata* has been realized.

Is there not in the method thus illustrated a suggestion worth putting to the uses of literature? May not the young be led to a true perception of literary values by just this process of smoothing the ways that lead to a correct taste, this device of fitting the conscious achievement to the earlier unconscious one? Those having occasion to observe young people who are going through the educational mill know that literary taste and a genuine delight in 'the authors' are not common, that they are the exception rather than the rule. Yet most children have, in the earlier stages of their school life, some germ of literary appreciation that needs nothing more than careful nurture to be brought to flower in the later stages. But when they come to the serious study of literature in school or college, it presents itself to them as a part of the 'grind'; it must be pursued in a certain prescribed way, which is likely enough the wrong way; it is treated as if it were geometry or linguistics; and the needs of the individual are lost sight of in the application of the system.

It seems to us a fundamental principle that anything like rigidity in the methods employed for the teaching of literature and the development of literary taste will necessarily prove fatal to success. In physics or in philology, the 'course' is a perfectly rational device; it is of the essence of training in such subjects that the work should be logical in its development. The path of least resistance is in them the same, or nearly the same, for all normally constituted minds. It is obviously the path to be followed, and the treatment of a class *en bloc* becomes not only possible but desirable. With literature the case is very different, and the path of least resistance must be discovered for each individual separately. The imagination is a wayward faculty, and atrophy is likely to follow upon the attempt abruptly to divert it into channels other than those it listeth to seek. The facts of literature may be apprehended by the intellect thus constrained, but that emotional accompaniment which makes of literature a personal message to the individual, which enshrines it, along with music and religion, in the most sacred recesses of the soul, is not to be coerced. Mere didactics are as powerless to impart the message of literature as they are to impart the message of music or of religion. The reward of such an attempt may be theology or counterpoint, formal rhetoric or literary history; but not that spiritual glow which is the one thing worth the having, that kindling of the soul which comes, perhaps when least expected, with the hearing of some ineffable strain, or the reading of some lightning-tipped verse.

There are many, no doubt, poor in emotional endowment, and unresponsive to the finer spiritual vibrations aroused by the masterpieces of verbal art, to whom literature has hardly more meaning than nature had for the yokel of Wordsworth's hackneyed ballad. To one of this class, if he do not actually look upon Homer from the standpoint of Zoilus, or share in Iago's view of the character of Othello, it is at least true that the last agony of Lear is nothing more than the death of an old man; for him the solemn passing of Œdipus

'To the dark benign deep underworld, alone'

is only a sort of hocus-pocus, and his ears are deaf to the
> 'Sudden music of pure peace'

wherewith the stars seal the successive divisions of Dante's threefold song.

But even for such as these the case is not altogether hopeless. The appeal of literature to the human soul is so manifold that it must find in every nature some pipes ready to be played upon. Dull though the sense may seem, it is at some point waiting to be quickened. For literature is life itself, in quintessential expression; how then can it fail, in some of its many phases, to have both a meaning and a message for every human being? The earliest responsive vibrations may be rudimentary in character, and combined in the simplest of harmonies. The heart may first be stirred by some bit of sentiment that would be accounted cheap by a refined taste; the imagination may first be fired by some grotesque *Märchen*, or by some wildly improbable tale of romantic adventure. The ripest literary taste has such beginnings as these, and the surest appreciation of literature is built upon such a foundation. Between the child, made forgetful of his surroundings by the spell of 'Robinson Crusoe' or the 'Arabian Nights,' and the man, finding spiritual refreshment in Cervantes or Molière, renewed strength in Milton, or solace from grief in Tennyson, there is no real break; the delight of the child and the grave joy of the man are but different stages of the same growth, and the one is what makes possible the other.

How far this development may go is a problem to be worked out for each individual separately; and there are doubtless, in each case, distinct limitations. What we have sought to emphasize is just this individual nature of the problem, and the fact that regimentation offers no solution that can be accounted satisfactory. The approach to literature is, in our current educational systems, hedged about with so many thorny obstructions that not a few young persons start bravely upon it only to fall by the way, disheartened at sight of the forbidding barriers erected by historical, linguistic, and metrical science, for the purpose of taking toll of all wayfarers. Whatever the usefulness for discipline of such subjects, the spirit of literature is not to be acquired by making chronological tables, or tracing the genealogies of words, or working out the law of decreasing predication. We may even sympathize to some extent with those who so revolt from all such methods as to refuse literature any place in the educational scheme. Turn the young person loose, they advise, in a well-stocked library, and let him develop his own tastes in his own way. He will make mistakes, they admit; there will be false starts not quickly righted; but there will be, in the long run, a wholesome development of taste, and a steady ascent to higher levels of appreciation. In any case, assimilation will not be forced, and conventional judgments will not be made to parade as personal convictions. This view has the one great merit of allowing full scope to individualism, but to admit that it speaks the last word would be to abandon altogether the position that educational theory is bound to maintain. That the young may profit by the guidance of the older and wiser is as true in literature as it is in any other of the great intellectual concerns. But the needs of the individual must be recognized as they are not now recognized, if literature is to play its proper part in education. Each case must be made the subject of a special diagnosis and a special prescription. We might apply to this problem the favorite formula of one of the schools of modern socialism: 'From every man according to his ability; to every man according to his needs'—although it is curious to see a socialist precept doing service in an individualist cause.

THE TEACHING OF LITERATURE.

THE methods made use of by our schools in the teaching of English literature have, for some years past, been in a transition stage, exhibiting a strong tendency toward more enlightened ways of dealing with this vastly important subject. The ferment is of the healthful type, and a fairly clarified product may not unreasonably be expected to result. When Matthew Arnold declared the future of poetry to be immense, he expressed a truth whose full significance may be realized only upon considerable reflection and the assumption of a broadly philosophical standpoint from which to view the coming conquests of culture. The same idea was expressed, with something of humorous exaggeration, by the author of 'The New Republic,' in attributing to John Stuart Mill the opinion that 'when all the greater evils of human life shall have been removed, the human race is to find its chief enjoyment in reading Wordsworth's poetry.' To indicate the importance of a due appreciation of literature we hardly need, upon this occasion, to repeat the hackneyed quotations in praise of books, from Richard de Bury to Carlyle; we may surely take it for granted that, allowing Arnold's demand on behalf of conduct, for a good three-fourths of our life, a considerable share of the remaining fraction may be claimed for literature. But if literature is to count for so much among our higher interests, the manner in which we set about to prepare the way for it is surely of the utmost importance, and any misdirection of energy in this preparation means an almost incalculable loss.

The main reliance of primary education, in this important subject, has been, and still is, the 'reader,' supplemented by occasional outside passages of prose and verse, generally selected without judgment, and committed to memory for the purpose of being 'spoken.' All 'readers' are bad in the sense that their use implies a very narrow limitation of the amount of matter to be read, and most of them are bad as regards the character of the selections included. The essential points to be insisted upon in the reading of lower schools are two, and two only. Nothing, absolutely nothing, should be read or recited that is not literature, and the amount of reading done by the child should be as large as possible. An ideal 'reader' might easily be compiled; indeed, excellent books of the sort are now to be had. But the use of the 'reader' generally means wearisome repetition of a limited amount of matter, whereas a rational method would demand very little repetition. The jaded interest with which a hapless child cons the familiar and well-thumbed pages is fatal to that appreciation of literature which it should be the first aim of primary education to encourage. Why, in these days of inexpensive production of reading-matter, should a child be forced to peruse the same pages over and over again, until the very sight of the book is hateful to him? Why should not every day bring to him fresh matter for the stimulation of his growing intelligence and imagination?

As for the other point upon which we should insist, the reading of nothing that is not worth reading, there can be no possible excuse for the kind of pabulum that is too commonly fed, by spoonfuls, to the mind of the young. When we consider the peculiarly receptive quality of the child's mind, the retentiveness whose loss he will so soon have occasion to mourn, the imagination so early to be dulled by the prosaic years to come, does it not seem a crime to make of these faculties or powers anything less than the utmost possible, to force the free spirit into ruts and waste it upon inanities? Having at hand the ample literature which gives expression to the childhood of the race, the literature of myth and fable, of generous impulse moving to heroic deed, how can a teacher be justified in substituting for this the manufactured and self-conscious twaddle that is the staple of most modern writing for children? Even for the very youngest who can read at all, there is no lack of suitable material. The melodies of Mother Goose, as Mr. Scudder has convincingly argued, are literature in a certain sense, surely in a far higher sense than the nursery jingles that too often take their place. And when a more advanced stage has been reached, there is the whole world of fairy lore, the wealth of religious and secular story-telling, the inexhaustible fund of historical incident, all of which must be included in the outfit of the adult mind, and much of which is better acquired at an early age than at any other. The child who has grown up in ignorance of the labors of Hercules and Siegfried's fight with the dragon, of the wanderings of Ulysses and the deeds of King Arthur, of Horatius at the bridge and Leonidas at Thermopylæ, has missed something that cannot be given him later, and may justly feel himself defrauded of a part of his birthright. The sense of injury is only aggravated by finding the mind filled instead with lumber worse than useless, with recollections of the worthless stuff, only too well remembered, that in childhood usurped the place that should have been filled by literature carefully selected for the value of its form or of its subject-matter.

While there are indications of an approaching reform in the methods of reading employed by our lower schools, and of reform along the lines above drawn, the progress in this direction will probably be so slow as to discourage all but the most sanguine. As long as the management of our common schools remains in the hands of persons selected with little or no reference to their fitness for the work — and that this is generally the case throughout the United States is a fact that need hardly be enlarged upon — we cannot hope for very much. In the fields of secondary and still higher education the outlook is brighter, for the problem is being dealt with in a more enlightened spirit. But the complaint that a considerable proportion of high school and college students have no literary aptitude whatever is still heard, and benumbs the efforts of many among the well-meaning, some of whom seem disposed to accept this proposition as a statement of one of the stubborn facts of nature. To our mind, the proportion will remain large as long as we do not attack the difficulty at its root in the very earliest years of school life. But we do not believe that there is any good evidence of the proportion being large by nature. It is not, however, surprising, when we consider the systematic way in which the literary appreciation is dulled by the narrow and mechanical methods of so much of our primary education, that the healthful growth of this faculty, thus arrested at a critical stage, should in many cases be found difficult or impossible of stimulation at a later period.

In secondary education, the old-fashioned treatment of English literature found its embodiment in a historical text-book, to be learned mostly by heart, accompanied sometimes by a hand-book of 'extracts,' in which each representative writer received an allotment of two or three pages. Sometimes the history and the 'extracts' were jumbled together, to the still further abridgment of the latter. The modern method, which has gained much ground of late, concentrates the attention upon a few longer works and their writers. This method is doubtless an advance upon the other, yet it sometimes means a reaction carried to extremes. We cannot afford to eliminate the historical text-book altogether, but we do need to have the right kind of book and to use it with intelligence. For the book that gives cut-and-dried critical formulas — a too prevalent type — the educator can have no use. What he wants is a book that shall stimulate the critical faculty in the student, not suppress it by supplying criticism ready-made. To direct, but not to force, opinion, and to encourage the widest range of independent reading, should be the aims of secondary instruction in literature. As for the bare facts—dates, historical conditions, and the like—they must be learned as facts, but they are not all as lifeless as many students think them, and a judicious and sympathetic instructor will succeed in clothing many of them with such associations as to make their retention an easy matter.

In college education, the reaction against the formal and dispiriting methods of the past has been very pronounced, and the study of literature appears to be in a state of generally healthful activity. In this field of education, the chief danger seems to lie in an undue preponderance of the scientific spirit. The temptation to regard works of literature as material for minute philological and historical analysis is very strong, and this procedure finds a certain warrant in the marked success which everywhere attends it. But the real question is whether the success thus obtained is of the sort to be desired. Does it not mean the intrusion of science upon a domain set apart for other, if not higher, purposes? It is doubtless much easier to treat literature by the method of science than by the method of æsthetics; but does not literature, thus treated, cease to assert its peculiar and indispensable function? Perhaps it may be just as well, as the late Edward T. McLaughlin suggested, to defer 'laboratory work' in literature 'until scientists introduce literary methods into the laboratory.' The effects of this 'mechanical and harshly intellectualized study' are not unfairly described by the writer in the following suggestive passage :

'If the literary neophyte's attention is directed too largely toward facts, he may mistake the means for the end, and as a result of his training find the principal object that confronts him as he takes up new works, nothing spiritual and æsthetic, but only the task of obtaining exterior information, hunting down quotations, dates, and allusions, surveying a poem by the rod and line of a technical phraseology, detecting parallels, and baying at the holes of conjectural originals, finally to emerge from his studies learned, but not literary.'

It seems to us that our colleges should no longer permit this sort of work to masquerade as the study of literature, but should relegate it to the department of science, where it properly belongs. But many of our college calendars, upon compliance with this demand, would be shown completely denuded of literary courses, which, in turn, might result in the much-needed provision for the study of literature in the true sense. It is no easy matter to disentangle the study of literature, thus conceived, from the meshes that philological and historical science have woven about it, but a few men have been successful in the work, and their example is there for the rest to follow. Men of this class, more than of any other, are needed by our colleges to-day; and in securing such men, giving free scope to their activity, and recognizing the claims of their work as no less serious than the claims of work in any other department, the colleges will do literature the best service in their power.

DEMOCRACY AND EDUCATION.

THE coming of democracy was the sign most clearly set in the social skies of our century at its dawn, and the triumph of the democratic spirit is the social phenomenon that stands out most distinctly as we look back upon the century's course. From our present point of vantage, indeed, the democracy whose successive conquests the years have marked is a very different thing from the democracy prefigured in the vision of those generous and ardent souls by whom its advent was hailed. The social ideal that once gave inspiration to the impassioned song of Shelley has become, in our own days, the not unfit recipient of the blatant laudation of Mr. Andrew Carnegie and his like. We now find no difficulty in seeing what the enthusiasm of the early nineteenth century could not see, the fact that the coming of democracy meant a revolution farther-reaching than any merely political revolution of former centuries had been, and the other fact that the democratic reconstruction of society was, in its full meaning and effect, incalculable by any method of social astrology known to men. The virtues of democracy were alone foreseen; its failings were left to be revealed by experience. Some of its sponsors, like Shelley, found early graves, dying happy in the faith. Others, like Wordsworth, lived to grow disheartened by the excesses of democracy, and sought for solace in new and sterile ideals. A few, like Landor, Mazzini, and Hugo, of faith too robust to be broken by adversity, held fast to the democratic principle, devoting themselves unswervingly to its service, never forgetting that through thorn-set ways alone men reach the stars.

The great poet who, more than any other, has linked with our own the early age of hope, must, on the whole, be reckoned with those in whom the faith, although it may have faltered, has not failed. That 'God fulfils himself in many ways' was his often repeated message to those who were impatient because the fulfilment was not immediate and in one particular way. He who told us, half a century ago, of his 'Vision of the

World,' who sounded the true note of democracy in the verses,

'Men, my brothers, men the workers, ever reaping something new :
That which they have done but earnest of the things that they shall do,'

never really departed from the principle then expressed. There may, it is true, be detected a note of pessimism in some of Tennyson's later poems, but it is not the absolute pessimism that despairs of the future. With the old age of our century, to those who have grown wise with its teachings, the problem of democracy has shown itself to be one of ever-increasing complexity, and the solution of that problem seems no longer near at hand.

'Forward far and far from here is all the hope of eighty years'

is a cry that still speaks of hope, if of hope deferred in heartsickening degree. The future belongs to democracy, and is a future of fair final promise, yet the way to it is both dark and devious, and will doubtless lead through many disappointments, and offer many phases of retrograde development. We may still confidently take 'Forward' as our watchword, but must

> 'Still remember how the course of time will swerve, Crook and turn upon itself in many a backward streaming curve.'

At present, it must seem to the most thoughtful that democracy is in danger of becoming, if it has not already become, a mere 'tyranny of the majority.' That the voice of the people is the voice of God is a dictum true within certain limits, true in its relation to the broad features of social organization, but profoundly false when applied to the special problems of society. For the solution of the special problem we must look to the expert; and the untrained masses, however praiseworthy their intention, can be expected to solve such problems only in a blundering and probably disastrous fashion. Only in an ideal society, a society that should have eliminated the 'remnant' by growth to the 'remnant' level of intelligence and culture, could the *vox populi* safely be left to decide upon the delicate questions of education, economics, and social ethics that somehow have to be decided by and for the people as a whole. Even the Athenian democracy, far surpassing any modern democracy in versatile capabilities and intelligence, made sad work of some of the special problems that it was called upon to solve.

The lesson above all others, then, that democracy has yet to learn, is the lesson of restraint. No doubt
> 'It is excellent
> To have a giant's strength, but it is tyrannous
> To use it like a giant.'

In the first flush of conscious power, it is not surprising that our nineteenth century democracy should have sought to regulate all sorts of matters that really call for the trained judgment of the specialist. The democracy of the twentieth century will, we trust, choose the wiser part of delegating its powers to agents specially chosen with regard to fitness for special work. It will realize the unspeakable foolishness of submitting scientific questions to popular vote. It will abandon the detestable practice of requiring its representatives to act as mere automata, and will instead choose them for their wisdom and leave them to act according to its dictates.

This may seem a hopelessly optimistic forecast, yet upon its eventuation the future of civilization depends. In spite of its manifold successes, democracy is still upon trial, and those who gird against it, from Carlyle to Maine, rightly fix upon the tendency above described as the most vulnerable feature of popular government. The history of our own country is particularly rich in illustrations of democratic ineptitude or failure, and so is peculiarly instructive to the student of political institutions. We have settled too many questions calling for extensive knowledge and ripe judgment by the rough method of the popular vote. Much of our public policy, so far as it has to do with economics and finance, has thus been shaped in direct defiance of the fundamental principles of those subjects, bringing upon ourselves disaster, and earning for us the mingled amusement and contempt of other countries. If the vagaries of our economic legislation have thus contributed to the gaiety of nations, the way in which we have dealt with our international complications has contributed to their righteous indignation.

Perhaps the most searching test of our democracy will be supplied by its attitude toward public education. Fortunately, the Constitution of our

Federal Government does not permit of educational centralization, and so makes a dull uniformity impossible. We shall always have instructive contrasts in systems and methods, and with them a constant spur to progress. Yet the centralization possible within the limits of the state, or even of the large city, has its dangers, and it too often happens that the educational forces of a considerable community are controlled by ignorance, and made ineffective by deference to uneducated opinion. Many of our state universities and the public schools of many of our large cities have to make all sorts of concessions to the spirit that insists upon a narrow practicality in education, and that almost wholly ignores the real objects of school and college training. State legislatures are never, and city school boards are rarely, composed of persons fit to exercise judgment in technical questions of education; yet these bodies are constantly engaged in meddlesome efforts to nullify the work of the professional educators whom they employ, and to whom, having once delegated the necessary authority, they should leave the most complete freedom of action. Such matters as the selection of teachers and of text-books, of the arrangement of curricula and the conditions of promotion and graduation, should, as a matter of course, be left to professional educators. When we consider the fact that these matters are, nevertheless, very generally controlled by political boards and legislatures, it is surprising that our schools and colleges should have made as creditable a record as they have succeeded in doing. It is not long since the Governor of Illinois publicly scoffed at the best educational ideals that the experience of the ages has established; and at about the same time a crusade of ignorance, led by the newspapers, threatened to seriously cripple the work of public education in Chicago.

When such occurrences have to be chronicled, it is clear that democracy has yet to learn its most important lesson. But it will not do to say that our century was not ready for the democratic experiment. The analogy between the individual and the nation is always a valuable one, and in application to this case its teaching is clear that only in the hard school of experience is real growth to be secured. If only the nation were as quick as the individual to profit by the teachings of experience! But the lessons are so soon forgotten, the nation is so wont to recur to the old sickening round of delusion, folly, and disaster, that only the most sanguine souls can steadfastly resist the promptings of despair and look forward with unabated confidence to the reign of reason and intelligence in which all the hopes of democracy must be centred.

THE FUTURE OF AMERICAN SPEECH.

THE coming conquests of the English language constitute a theme much favored in the discussions of debating societies and the orations of college commencements. With anyone born to our English speech it must, indeed, be a matter of pride that the language of Shakespeare should have won a secure foothold in North America and South Africa, in India, in Australia, and in the Isles of the Sea. But the pride thus gratified by a superficial view of the growth already achieved and the growth probably to be recorded in the years to come is tempered when, upon closer observation, we realize that this extension in area of the English language is likely to have deterioration in quality for a concomitant. However desirable may be the increased use of our language by the nations of the earth, we cannot regard with equanimity the tendency of the language, in its territorial extensions, to assume corrupt dialectic forms.

The power of literature to give fixity to speech is very great, but we cannot blindly count upon it for the impossible. The language of Italy was cast in definite mould by the genius of Dante, and it still retains the impress given it six centuries ago, but we must recollect that this language has never been called upon to meet the test of transplantation to another soil, and adoption by a mixed, and in part, therefore, an alien race. So the English language, in its native environment, is still substantially the language fixed by Chaucer and Shakespeare, but observers are not wanting who declare that the English language, transplanted to the American continent, is undergoing radical changes, and becoming a dialect of the parent form of speech. Of course we are not to expect anything like a repetition of the process by which the Latin language, crossing Alps and Pyrenees, underwent first corruption and then transformation. The solidarity of modern civilization makes that impossible. All countries having a common language are linked together by bonds that will never permit the speech of one to become unintelligible to the inhabitants of the other.

But, while retaining a common intelligibility, it is quite possible for the offsets of our language to become so differentiated one from the other that they may fairly be described as dialects, and this is a danger which everyone familiar with what is best and noblest in our common literary inheritance will be quick to appreciate. We do not now refer to the incorporation of those new words made necessary by a new environment, and illustrated by the Pacific Coast stories of Mr. Harte, the Indian tales of Mr. Kipling, and the novels and poems of Australian writers. Nor do we refer to those developments of idiom taken on by all living languages, and the necessary sign of their vitality. But we do refer to the mushroom growths of speech that spring up everywhere among us, the modes of expression that result from mere slovenliness of mind, and find no warrant either in the genius of the language or in the necessities of the situation. These linguistic abortions are encouraged by a press unworthy of its function because unfaithful to its trust, and accepted by an easy-going and uncritical public, too eager in its desire for the new thing, and too heedless in its tolerance of the short cut which generally means incomplete expression, of the barbarism which usually defeats the very purpose of expression.

The language that is spoken by the people of this country is the language that is read in their popular literature — in their newspapers, magazines, and paper-covered novels — and is not a language in which they have reason to take pride. A great share of the writing done for our newspapers is done by uneducated persons, and offends every instinct of literary decency. A higher standard is offered by the best of our magazines, but few can resist the temptation of a well-known name, and any sort of notoriety is a passport to the pages of all but three or four of them. The oldest and for many years the most dignified of our reviews has been degraded to the level of the sensational daily paper, and offers to its readers of to-day as few well-written pages as it offered of ill-written pages to its readers of a generation ago. Of the kind of English in which most of our popular novels are written the less that is said the better. But we may remark that the realistic tendency of recent fiction has to answer, among many other sins, for that of fastening upon the minds of its readers the grossest solecisms of uneducated speech. Anything is permissible in the conversations of its characters, for is it not the function of Realism to represent people as they act and speak? So the illiterate writer has only to select his types of characters from the uneducated crowd, and is then free to pen the sort of English to which he is accustomed. If, by chance, the 'piebald jargon' which he places upon their lips passes over into the descriptive and other passages in which the writer speaks for himself, the average reader will hold the offence of little weight, if it even attracts his attention.

The degradation of the American language from the high standard still measurably preserved in the parent country is a phenomenon of the gravest significance. We are not now concerned with the quibbling about 'Americanisms' and 'Briticisms' that has supplied amusement to many ingenious controversialists. There is about as much to say upon one side of that question as upon the other, and the game appears to be drawn. The question now before us is not that of certain objectionable locutions — whether their origin be English or American; it is the far more serious question of how far the American language has become an inferior dialect of the English. Those of our writers who resent any imputation of this sort usually ignore the real question altogether. They seek to divert attention from it either by childish *tu quoque* arguments, or by resort to vague generalizations upon the fluctuations to which all living languages are subject. They eloquently oppose 'the wild flowers of speech, plucked betimes with the dew still on them, humble and homely and touching,' to 'the waxen petals of rhetoric as a schoolmaster arranges them.' To the writer who has arrayed for us these touchingly contrasted figures 'the grammarian, the purist, the pernicketty stickler for trifles, is the deadly foe of good English, rich in idioms and racy of the soil.' That American English is, on the whole, as good as any other, that its peculiarities are but the evidences of a healthful vitality, is the sum of the plea urged by these zealous linguistic patriots.

But the question is not to be thus flippantly disposed of. Dr. Fitzedward Hall, who is, we must remember, an American, although he has lived in England for many years, replies to the sort of apologists above cited in the following emphatic terms: 'With those who, either from denseness of ignorance or from æsthetic insensibility, deliver themselves in this uncritical fashion, it would be squandering words to argue: they must be left to perish in their pravity.' And he goes on to say: 'More or less, as much as the language of Scotland, American English, as a whole, has already come to be a dialect; and day by day it entitles itself more and more to that designation.' These quotations are taken from an article published by Dr. Hall in the London 'Academy' after it had been declined by 'two American periodicals.' The greater part of the article is devoted to a list of 'locutions which go far to realize finished debasement,' taken from a book by one of our better American writers. Although exception may be taken to some of Dr. Hall's illustrations, the majority of them are clearly examples of bad English. That it is difficult for an American to avoid writing bad English he freely admits, and the passage in which the admission is made, although somewhat long, is of so great interest that it deserves to be reproduced here in full.

'If egotism for a moment is pardonable, no false shame deters me from avowing that, though I have lived away from America upwards of forty-six years, I feel, to this hour, in writing English that I am writing a foreign language, and that, if not incessantly on my guard, I am in peril of stumbling. Nor will it be amiss for any American, when experimenting like myself, to feel as I do, and never to relax his vigilance, if he would not every now and then reveal himself, needlessly and to his prejudice, as an exotic. Not for five minutes can he listen to the conversation of his fellow-countrymen, or for that length of time read one of their newspapers, or one of such books as they usually write, without exposure to the influence of some expression which is not standard English. Try as he will to resist this influence, successful resistance to it is well-nigh impossible. On the other hand, if he is indifferent about resisting it, his fancied English will, a thousand to one, be chequered with solecisms, crudenesses, and piebald jargon, of the sort which the pages of Mrs. Stowe, Mr. E. P. Roe, and Mr. Howells have rendered familiar. In short, the language of an American is, all but inevitably, more or less dialectal.'

That Dr. Hall speaks with authority few will be bold enough to dispute. And, although he does not suggest any definite remedy for the insidious disease that has attacked our language, he clearly believes that remedies are yet available.

A century from now, he says, our population will be several times that of Great Britain.

'Circumstances generated by unprecedented combinations have entailed on us a recognizable dialect, and one which is rapidly developing. Whether it is fated to remain a dialect is a hazardous speculation. Yet, unless we chance to breed a matter of half a dozen Shakespeares and Miltons, it will hardly, without great purification, reach the dignity of a substantive language. But, be its eventual status what it may, that which should especially weigh with us is its unquestionable destiny to serve as the mother-tongue of hundreds of millions. Towards the shaping of it, so that our successors shall do us credit, we can contribute consciously. Most surely it behoves us, therefore, to take measures, and take them promptly, to the end that, so far as may prove feasible, its evolution be controlled by proficients in knowledge and taste, and not by sciolists and vulgarians.'

What these measures should be, we are left to determine. Half a century ago, writing, *mutatis mutandis*, upon the same subject, Schopenhauer proposed in all seriousness that the State should take a hand in the matter, and establish a system of linguistic censorship of the press, with penalties for the misuse of words, for syntactical errors, and for ' impudent mockery of grammar.' ' Is the German language outlawed?' he exclaimed, ' too insignificant to deserve the legal protection enjoyed by every dung-hill?' So heroic a remedy as this is hardly within our reach, and we must look for aid to educational systems rather than to legislatures. By wisely directed education, and by that alone, may we hope to come once more into secure possession of the rich heritage, so nearly lost, of the speech of Shakespeare and of Tennyson. To accomplish this we must improve the methods of our elementary education, and must make our higher education higher still. We must strengthen at all points the study of the English languages and literature; we must insist upon the acquaintance, from childhood up, with only good models of style; we must make the proper expression of thought, in every department of work, an aim concurrent with that of acquiring the special subject-matter of the study pursued.

THE USE AND ABUSE OF DIALECT.

THERE are indications — not very marked as yet, but still indications — that the day of the dialect versifier and story-teller is waning. The literary epidemic for which he is responsible has raged with unabated virulence in this country for the past ten years or more. It has had almost complete possession of the *bric-a-brac* popular magazine. Its contagion has even extended to those periodicals which we too fondly fancied to stand for the dignities, as opposed to the freaks, of literature. At the other extreme, it has been disseminated and vulgarized by the newspaper and the popular reciter. A few of the men and women whom we count as real forces in American letters have been numbered among its victims. But all epidemics exhaust themselves in time, and we are encouraged to believe that this one is nearly spent. A tabulation of the contents of our popular magazines would now, we think, show a smaller proportion of pages unreadable for their bad spelling than would have been disclosed by a similar investigation made two years ago. The journalist, having for a time done his best to spread the fashion of dialect, is now aiming at it the shafts of his dull yet not ineffective satire. Many a literary worker is beginning to suspect that to misspell as many words as possible is not exactly the noblest of ambitions. Best of all, the whole fabric of realism—that is, of the crude photographic realism so noisily trumpeted by its defenders—is crumbling away, to make room in due time, we trust, for the true realism of the masters; and with this fabric there falls whatever theoretical defense of the dialect poem or novel may heretofore have seemed plausible.

We by no means anticipate the complete disappearance of the dialect element from our imaginative literature, nor would such a reaction be desirable. But we do expect the time to come when dialect shall occupy its proper place in composition, and be treated as a means rather than as an end. There is an important distinction between the story written for the sake of dialect and the use of dialect for the sake of the story; the latter practice is as excusable or even praiseworthy as the former is reprehensible. The question is one between a writer and his own conscience. Let the story-teller ask himself this question: Is it my purpose to produce a faithful yet idealized transcript of life, with its joys and its sorrows, with its tender human relationships and its grim struggle for the mastery of adverse conditions, the use of dialect being one of the elements necessary to the representation of essential truth; or am I merely taking advantage of a current fashion that tends to degrade the literary art, and, making of a grotesque orthography the *raison d'être* of my work, adding just enough of description and fancy and pathos to give my work the verisimilitude needed for it to pass muster at all? Most writers have sufficient conscience to answer this question truthfully, if squarely put; if they shirk the answer for themselves, they may be sure that the public, sooner or later, will find it for them. And the ultimate verdict of the only public worth writing for will never be favorable to the workman who fails to recognize the imperative obligation of this higher sort of conscientiousness.

When used with discrimination and artistic

restraint, dialect is, of course, an admissible element in both poetry and fiction. English literature would be far the poorer without the treasures of Scotch dialect preserved in the poems of Burns and the novels of the author of 'Waverley.' Likewise, we could ill spare the work of the Provençal poets from the literature of France, of Goldoni's Venetian comedies from that of Italy, or of Reuter's Plattdeutsch tales from that of Germany. In all these cases, the work simply could not have been done at all without the employment of dialect; yet no one would venture to assert that the exploitation of a dialect was the prime motive that led to the composition of 'Tam O'Shanter' or 'The Antiquary,' of 'Miréio' or 'Il Carnovale di Venezia' or 'Ut Mine Stromtid.' These are all instances of a richly endowed artistic nature finding expression in the medium most natural for his purpose. Even in our own country, a similar plea may be made for the language of Hosea Biglow, or of Mr. Cable's creoles, or of Miss Murfree's Tennessee mountaineers. But the swarm of commonplace and uninspired scribblers of dialect that have descended upon our periodical press during the past decade need not hope to find a safe refuge in the shadow of such really significant names as have been cited; their pretensions are too utterly without warrant and their productions too entirely without justification. Not Lowell, but 'Josh Billings,' is their model and Great Example.

No discussion of the abuse of dialect that should omit the educational view would be adequate. The corrupting influence that may hardly be escaped by adult readers is tenfold more serious in its effect upon the growing mind. The prevalence of dialect in the papers and magazines that provide young people with most of their reading puts a new and formidable difficulty in the way of teachers and parents. Even the books put into our schools as models for the guidance of the young—the school 'readers' themselves—often contain examples of perverted diction that cannot fail to exert an evil influence upon the impressionable years of childhood. Upon this aspect of our subject, we cannot do better than quote some pointed observations from a paper by Professor Willis Boughton, of Ohio University. Mr. Boughton says:

'For the past decade some of our most popular periodicals have been furnishing their readers with a weekly or monthly diet of dialect stories. A handful of editors have declared that the people want such literature, and it is produced. Instead of romances in cultivated language, we are introduced to most ordinary characters who use most ordinary folk lore. The Christmas story, Mr. Howells asserts, is written in the "Yankee dialect and its Western modifications." Even our verse is corrupted. Notice a stanza reproduced from a leading magazine :

"I'm been a visitin' 'bout a week
To my little cousin's at Nameless Creek,
An' I'm got the hives an' a new straw hat
An' I'm come back home where my beau lives at."

What literature! If the magazine, one of the greatest educational factors in our country, will tolerate such language; if you and I read it, and smile at it, and quote it, the Cincinnati teacher may be pardoned for the use of language that shocked Dr. Rice. To preserve the speech of a vanishing people, dialect literature may be justified; but to propagate such language is vicious. At school, the teacher may dwell at length upon the linguistic beauties of the "Village Blacksmith"; but on Friday afternoon some urchin declaims :

"The Gobble-uns' 'ill git you
Ef you don't watch out,"

and soon all the children in the district are repeating his words. Why the offspring of even polite society are prone to use bad English need be no longer a matter of wonder.'

'To propagate such language is vicious.' The words are none too strong, and we thank Mr. Boughton for them, hoping that the protest he raises will be echoed by educators everywhere.

These are some of the abuses of dialect; what, then, are its uses? To what fruitful end may we divert the effort now worse than wasted by the dialect-mongers of our periodical literature? By substituting a scientific for an artistic purpose, by making a serious study of dialect instead of playing with it. The facts of dialect speech, as distinguished from the inventions of the newspaper humorist, are of great importance to the history of language. No more important linguistic work remains to be done in this country than that of recording the thousands of local variations of our speech from what may be called standard English. To fix these colloquialisms in time and place, to trace them to their origins, to construct speech-maps embodying the salient facts of popular usage wherever it has distinctive features — these are scientific aims of the worthiest. Work of this sort is being energetically carried on by a constantly-increasing number of observers in this country; but the ranks still call for additions, and new-comers will be heartily welcomed. As a coördinating agency for such scattered contributions to knowledge, the American Dialect Society, founded in 1889, is, in a quiet way, establishing important scientific conclusions. The lay observer is hardly competent to make the finer distinctions in pronunciation that come within the scope of the trained phonetician, but he can be extremely useful in the collection of vocabularies. The Society asks him to do two things for each peculiar word or idiom that comes to his notice — 'first, to fix the fact that it occurs in dialect usage in a sense differing from standard English, and, secondly, to fix the local limits of this usage.' All such variations from the normal ' represent just the class of facts on which the scientific study of language rests. Many of them are survivals from older periods of the language; many new words are formed or adopted to meet a real need arising from new conditions, and so ultimately gain a place in standard English; and many variations in pronunciation illustrate phonetic changes which are constantly going on in language development. The philologist needs to know, from a more reliable source than the ordinary novelist furnishes, the exact locality where each word or phrase is used (implying, also, a knowledge of where it is not used); just what it means to those who use it, and what local variations there are, if any, in its form and meaning; just when each new word came in or old one went out of use.' If, perchance, our little sermon on the use and abuse of dialect should turn even one misguided realist from a grinder-out of dialect ' copy ' for the newspapers into an exact observer of local usage for the scientific purposes of the Society, it will not have been preached in vain.

READING AND EDUCATION.

In these days of multiplied universities and degrees, when a young man or woman of earnest purpose is rarely so handicapped by adverse environment as to be quite unable to get the higher education in the academic sense of that term, it is possible that we attach too much importance to the culture that is based purely upon scholastic titles. Historical examples without end prove to us that culture of the finest type has been attainable outside the walls of any institution of learning, and there is no reason to doubt that the process which has produced self-educated men in the past is equally available and effective at the present time. Indeed, it may be urged that the man intellectually self-made, if his achievement show him to be really educated, has an advantage over the man who has found the ways of learning smoothed for him, the rough places levelled, and the natural impediments to progress cleared away by other hands than his own. It is he who best knows the value of what has been so hardly acquired; his attainment has a substance and a solidity that the most brilliant of university careers may fail to give. After all, the test of culture, outside of narrow academic circles, is not based upon such external things as degrees and fellowships, but upon capacity, upon evidence of the finer issues of thought and feeling, and the power to quicken other spirits to those issues.

Perhaps the most important of educational institutions is that which everyone may have at his door, or even within arm's reach—a well filled set of book-shelves. Having this, we have, however socially isolated, the 'means of getting to know, on all matters which most concern us, the best which has been thought and said in the world.' One is almost ashamed to make so hackneyed a phrase do duty once more, but Matthew Arnold seized the root of the matter, and if the thing needs to be repeated at all, it can hardly be done otherwise than in his words. Reading is a very serious affair, one of the most serious that there are; yet how few realize both in thought and act its educational possibilities. A man's library, assuming it to be for use and not for display, is a better index to his character than the most detailed of external biographies. Show us the man at work in his library, and we view him in his essence, not in his seeming. There is no greater educational problem than that of persuading men and women everywhere—not merely the few favored by training and predisposition — to surround themselves with books of the right sort, and to make the right use of them. Our popular educational movements, our Chautauqua circles and University Extension courses, are all working in this direction, although rather aimlessly and with much misdirection of energy; what we need is more persistent and systematic endeavor — effort duly elastic and individual in adaptation while still systematic — on the part of all who are occupied with the diverse phases of the educational movement. Every teacher, every librarian, every popular lecturer, every writer for magazine or newspaper, can do something for the common cause by way of influence; every private individual, in his own circle of acquaintances, can at least do something by way of example.

The average adult, whose intellectual environment seems to be a matter of choice, is really subjected to influences that are not easy to resist. The modern newspaper, with its bad writing and its vulgar ideals, the popular magazine, with its ephemeral or sensational programme, the cheap book, even cheaper in its contents than in its mechanical execution — these are the temptations that beset his every spare hour, and deprive him of communion with the great spirits who stand ready to tell him ' the best which has been thought and said in the world.' 'Will you go and gossip with your housemaid or your stable-boy, when you may talk with queens and kings; or flatter yourself that it is with any worthy consciousness of your own claims to respect that you jostle with the hungry and common crowd for *entrée* here, and audience there, while all the while this eternal court is open to you, with its society, wide as the world, multitudinous as its days,—the chosen and the mighty of every place and time?' None of us can altogether escape the distracting influence of the commonplace writing that on every hand insinuates itself into our acquaintance; yet if we content ourselves with such work, if we do not resolutely reject its impudent pretension of sufficiency, we miss the most effective means for the realization of our better selves. Every reader ought now and then to fortify himself against temptation by reading some such essay as Mr. Ruskin's on 'Kings' Treasuries,' or Mr. Morley's on 'The Study of Literature,' or Mr. Harrison's on 'The Choice of Books'—not for their commendation of particular lines of reading, or to blindly acquiesce in their individual *dicta*, but for their lofty standpoint, their liberal outlook, and their tonic effect.

The foundations of the reading habit are, of course, laid in childhood; and the responsibility for these foundations is one of the greatest that the professional educator has to bear. The child should be as carefully guided in the choice of his reading as the adult should be free to determine what is best for his own spiritual needs. How precious are the years from six to sixteen, with their eager receptivity and their retentive grasp, seems to be but imperfectly understood by the directors of our schools. It is hardly less than criminal to provide children of such an age with the namby-pamby artificial reading that is now manufactured for their use. A child's reading should be confined to the very best literature that he is capable of understanding — and it is astonishing what he will understand if given a chance. Nor should he be kept upon short rations for the purpose of drill in vocal expression. Fresh matter is always better than old for discipline, and the most vitalizing pages lose their power for good if too frequently conned. The childish desire for new worlds to conquer is very strong, and is sure to find vent in the wrong direction if not freely indulged in the right one.

The high school and college period of education is essentially that in which the student is trained to shift for himself. It is the period when restrictions upon reading must be relaxed, and freedom of choice watchfully encouraged. Somewhere within this period of intellectual adolescence there comes a transitional stage which tests all the training of the previous years. The duty of those who are responsible for the student during this critical period is rather to stimulate than to direct his reading; to encourage him in looking beyond the horizon of his text-books, to make it easy and pleasant for him to read in helpful lines; to throw all sorts of unobtrusive obstacles in his path, if he exhibits any tendency toward intellectual dissipation. The school or college library is, next to the wise instructor, an essential factor in this problem, and the studies of history and literature, of the ancient and modern languages, are those upon which reliance must mainly be placed in this task of making of formal education a real preparation for life. We have of late years witnessed a remarkable expansion in the scientific departments of school and college, and a greatly increased expenditure for their adjuncts of laboratory and museum. The expansion was needed, and no educator can intelligently begrudge it. But the group of studies which find in the library both museum and laboratory — the studies which we rightfully call humanities and for which we thereby claim the place of first importance and of closest relationship to our deepest spiritual needs — may fairly demand as much attention and as large an expenditure as the sciences of nature. It is not too much to ask that every dollar set apart for scientific apparatus shall be matched by another dollar set apart for literary apparatus. The student of history or of literature ought to have the use of his own set of books, just as the student of chemistry has the use of his own set of reägents. When the humanities come again into their own, this necessity will be recognized as fully as the necessity of laboratory teaching in chemistry is now recognized.

Given the right guidance in childhood, and the right influences during adolescence, the reading habit may be counted upon to remain a genuine educational influence through life. The importance of such guidance and such influences can hardly be over-estimated. But for those who have missed them, for those who in the future will miss them, there is still the consoling truth that serious aims coupled with earnest endeavor can nearly always find the path to a very complete culture. 'The best which has been thought and said in the world,' like the sunlight, shines freely for all, and to it the veriest mole may, if he will, grope his way. 'Reading maketh a full man,' and more than that no scheme of formal education, however extensive, may accomplish.

SUMMER READING.

THERE are many, doubtless, to whom the suggestion of a summer vacation largely devoted to reading, particularly if undertaken with profitable intent, will seem little better than a counsel of perfection. The strained nerves and the weary brain demand, they will urge, that whatever weeks or months may be annually snatched from the grasp of toil should be given up to recreation in its primitive sense, to the renewing of the exhausted vitality, to the rebuilding of the wasted tissue. At such times, the only books of which they will hear are those which the best authority tells us are to be found in running brooks, and the only sermons to which they are disposed to listen are the mute discourses of the stones upon sea-cliff or mountain-side. And there is undoubtedly a degree of tension, reached by many in our feverish latter-age, from which relief is only possible upon condition of a complete, if temporary, abandonment of civilization with all its devices.

We are impelled for a brief space to relapse into barbarism, and, seeking new strength by contact with the bare earth, to realize in our own experience the myth of Antæus.

But such relapses are not for long, and, the first joy of freedom and relaxation being at an end, the mental activities quickly reassert their need of occupation. The pendulum of life has soon swung all the way from the unendurable strain of daily recurrent labor to the equally unendurable *ennui* of prolonged idleness. The pure joy of existence may suffice for the moment, but the sense of vacuity sets in after awhile, and imperatively calls for some form of diversion that shall not leave Nature to do all the recreative work. At such times, more forcibly perhaps than at any others, books offer us their serviceable solace, and we congratulate ourselves upon the instinctive foresight that led us to provide ourselves with such companions. Then, reclining upon shaded lawn or veranda, upon deck or seashore or pine-clad mountain slope, fortified against the intrusions of care, and at peace with all the world, we enjoy in equal measure the ministries of Nature and of Art, as far removed from *ennui* as from toil, and the discords of life are resolved into the richest of harmonies.

What books are best suited to the needs of the long summer days? We have known a young man, in contemplation of an ocean voyage, to take with him the 'Kritik der Reinen Vernunft.' Luckily there was a library on the ship, and Kant remained undisturbed at the bottom of the traveller's trunk. On the other hand, there are too many people whose idea of a summer's literary provision becomes embodied in a package of ephemeral novels of varying degrees of unreality or imbecility, and an armful of illustrated periodicals. We hardly know which of the two extremes thus illustrated deserves the severer censure, but if either case is to have our sympathies it must be that of the Kantian student rather than that of the 'Dodo'-laden excursionist. The former, at least, has a rational motive, if his judgment be woefully at fault; the latter is, however unconsciously, doing his best to waste a golden opportunity.

The rational person will take neither Kant nor 'Dodo' to his place of summer resort, for he will know that there is a grateful mean between the substantial but not easily digestible quality of the one and the mere frothiness of the other. He will know, for one thing, that there is an abundance of literature which is of the very best, yet which makes no strenuous demand upon the faculties, which can hold the attention without conscious effort, so smooth is the flow and so harmonious the form. What reading, for example, could be more ideally fit for the long summer afternoons than the poetry of the 'Faërie Queene' or the 'Earthly Paradise,' the prose of the 'Pentameron' or 'Marius the Epicurean'? Such reading as this becomes a permanent intellectual possession, an influence moulding imagination and character, and the retrospective charm naturally attaching to the memory of a summer outing will be not a little enhanced by association with the imperishable beauty of such works of literary art. There is a passage in one of FitzGerald's letters which embodies the whole gospel of summer reading. He says:

'I am now a good deal about in a new Boat I have built, and thought (as Johnson took Cocker's Arithmetic with him on travel, because he shouldn't exhaust it) so I would take Dante and Homer with me, instead of Mudie's

Books, which I read through directly. I took Dante by way of slow Digestion: not having looked at him for some years: but I am glad to find I relish him as much as ever: he atones with the Sea; as you know does the Odyssey — these are the Men!'

What shall we do, then, with what Mr. Ruskin calls the good books of the hour — telling us that 'we ought to be entirely thankful for them, and entirely ashamed or ourselves if we make no good use of them'— if we are not to put them in our trunk when we start upon our vacation? We have no disposition to underrate the usefulness of 'these bright accounts of travels, good-humored and witty discussions of questions, lively or pathetic story-telling in the form of novel, firm fact-telling by the real agents concerned in the events of passing history.' But we think that the time for them is the hour left us after a hard day's work, or the occasional holiday, rather than the summer's weeks or months of continuous rest. When that happy season comes round, we can put it to better uses, and, if we are going to do any reading at all, it surely offers the occasion of occasions for that close acquaintance with 'the authors' that we can never hope to make during the ordinary routine of active life. If we are well-advised, we will leave the ephemeral and scrappy literature of the day for the day which brings it forth, and not allow it to usurp our attention during the only part of the year when we are really free to enter upon enjoyment of our great heritage of Books in the higher and better sense. 'Who would think of taking up the "Faërie Queene" for a stopgap?' while waiting for the sound of the dinner-bell, Lamb asks us. And, to point the obverse of the moral, let us in turn ask: Who would think, or who ought to think, of devoting the long summer days to books whose final cause is to supply us with stopgaps, and which, when put to other uses, are as much out of place as Spenser would be in the hungry half-hour preceding the evening repast?

THE SUMMER SCHOOL.

Observers of our educational activity cannot fail to have been impressed by the recent growth of the Summer School. The phase of educational work represented by that deserving institution attracts yearly more and more attention, and every recurrent summer season offers to the ambitious student a wider choice among places and subjects. In the earlier chapters of its history the outcome of private initiative, the organized forces of American education soon perceived the possibilities of the Summer School as a supplementary educational process, and now associate themselves unequivocally with its work. The imposing lists of gatherings more or less educational in character, published year by year in various periodicals, give some idea of the dimensions to which the work has grown, and even these lists are rarely complete. 'More than one hundred Summer Schools,' we were told in the spring of 1895, 'will be in active operation in the United States during the coming season.' Perhaps the best indication of the extent to which Summer Schools have become an accepted factor in our educational work is afforded by the Report of the United States Commissioner of Education for 1891–92, published by the Government Printing Office. For this Report, a special investigation of the subject of Summer Schools was made by Dr. W. W. Willoughby, and the results of that investigation may well be considered surprising even by those fairly familiar with the subject.

Every new educational movement finds dissenters, and there is involved in this growing utilization of the summer months for educational purposes a fundamental principle that cannot be altogether ignored. There are some who will see in the movement merely another indication of that hurry and unrest so characteristic of American life in its other phases, and who will claim that our summer vacations ought to be devoted to their primary purpose of relaxation and recreation. And there is no doubt that we need really to rest at times, to break the process of overstimulation, to give our weary nerves an opportunity to renew their dissipated energies. The best work is not, as a rule, done by those who toil for the greatest number of hours or days, but rather by those who so shape their lives as to maintain the working period at its highest potency. Yet it must not be forgotten, on the other hand, that the truest rest is not that of torpor or lethargy, but is rather to be sought in variety of interest or aim. And the Summer School, carried on as it usually is among the mountains or by lakeside and seashore, means for the most of us so complete a change of environment that it may bring recuperation to the tired brain even although that brain persist in the moderate exercise of its habitual function. At all events, the objections of the dissenter are minimized, and need not be taken very seriously. Some sympathy may indeed be demanded for the officers and instructors of the Summer School, since to them, more nearly than to the average student, the work done is a continuation of the kind of work they have been doing all the rest of the year, and the sacrifices they are called upon to make are not inconsiderable. There is something wrong about a system which pretends that nine or ten months of work are enough for the teacher, yet which compensates him so inadequately for that work as to force him to eke out his income by working on for the two or three months remaining. As long as any large proportion of the instruction in our Summer Schools is done by men thus compelled to do it, not only will the efficiency of the Summer School suffer, but the tone of the whole educational profession will remain lower than it ought to be.

Historically, the American Summer School begins with the establishment, in 1872, of the Zoological Laboratory on Penikese Island, under the direction of Louis Agassiz. That famous school, which had but two sessions, was the progenitor of the Chesapeake School of the Johns Hopkins University, the Schools at Annisquam, and Wood's Holl, and the school of the Brooklyn Institute on Long Island. These biological schools form a group by themselves, and no one can question the great importance of the work they have done in original research and the training of specialists. Allied to them are the schools forming the second group in Dr. Willoughby's classification, described as ' Summer Schools giving instruction in single subjects.' Towards this group the Concord School of Philosophy, opened in 1879, occupies the historical relation of the Penikese Laboratory to the schools of the biological group. The Concord School had ten annual sessions, the last of them, in 1888, being limited to an Alcott memorial service. Of its several successors, the most direct, if we take both spirit and organization into account, is the school conducted by Mr. Thomas Davidson, for a few years at Farmington, Connecticut, afterwards and still at a secluded spot in Keene Valley, New York, beautifully situated in the heart of the Adirondacks. It is now called the Glenmore School, and is devoted to the culture sciences. The Plymouth School of Applied Ethics, inaugurated in 1891, mainly through the efforts of Dr. Felix Adler, may also be considered here. It represents the highest scientific plane yet reached by the schools of this group, and its field and influence have broadened with every succeeding year of its existence. We have not space even to name the remaining schools devoted to special subjects, conspicuous among which are the many flourishing schools of music and the languages dotting the country from East to West. And we must also pass by without mention the countless summer institutes and other schools for the training of teachers that are every year pursuing their silent but effective work of raising the standard of the teaching profession in our country.

The Chautauqua system, with its ever broadening scope and its countless ramifications, must have a paragraph to itself. It is estimated that more than one person in every hundred of our entire population visits the yearly gatherings of the various schools organized upon the Chautauqua plan, if not directly controlled by its management. The beginnings of this system are to be looked for only about a score of years back. In 1874 occurred the first summer meeting on the shores of Lake Chautauqua, planned by Mr. Lewis Miller and Dr. John H. Vincent. From this first meeting, attended by some six hundred students from all parts of the country, there has sprung the system of popular education whose name is now a household word throughout the land. The Chautauqua Assembly proper provides a great variety of courses in history, literature, language, science, and pedagogics. The College of Liberal Arts, superadded in 1879, offers courses of a more exacting character, having much of the character of regular college work, and, like such work, leading to degrees that are not so lightly bestowed as some people imagine. Then there are the outlying Chautauqua assemblies, a numerous progeny, held in attractive spots scattered all over the country. More than sixty of these assemblies attest the fertility of the fundamental Chautauqua idea of combining instruction with recreation. It is easy to scoff at the work of these assemblies, and to point out the obvious fact that they are in no sense substitutes for the colleges proper; it is easy to visit any one of them, and have an eye for its vacation aspect alone; it is easy, also, to talk about scrappiness and superficiality; but all comment of this sort is beside the mark. No one can take a close view of the Chautauqua work without recognizing in it a very shrewd and practical application of possible means to a highly desirable end; no one can take a broad view of the work without seeing that it is a factor of appreciable importance in our educational life.

In conclusion, we must say a few words about the steadily increasing amount of summer work undertaken by the universities themselves, with the aid of their organization, equipment, and scientific methods. In a certain sense, the Penikese Laboratory of Agassiz should open this chapter of our history, for it was the evident utility of such an enterprise that led to the organization of the Harvard summer courses, which have, since 1874, formed a regular department of the work of that University. Scientific subjects have mainly occupied these courses, and the work has been chiefly planned to meet the needs of teachers. These Harvard courses emphasize the important principle that pedagogic instruction should not be purely theoretical, but should rather take up, although still with pedagogic intent, some concrete branch of knowledge, and, in teaching its substance, at the same time convey an acquaintance with the methods that its teachers should employ. The University of Virginia was also a pioneer in the work of Summer Schools, and its School of Law was started as early as 1870, although it remained in an embryonic state until 1875. One institution after another has since fallen into line, and summer work is now done at Cornell, Yale, Columbia, Stanford, and many of the State Universities of the West. The University Extension movement is also taking possession of the summer field, and such a programme as that offered for the summer of 1895 at the University of Pennsylvania is really extraordinary in its scope and interest. It remained, however, for the new University of Chicago first to occupy the position that the summer months are just as good as any others for full university work in all departments, and first to offer the example of a great institution of learning open to students from one end of the year to the other. The results of this undertaking all go to show that President Harper had reason to attach great importance to this unprecedented feature of the University planned by him. At a single bound this new educational departure passed from the experimental stage to the stage of successfully accomplished fact, and summer education entered upon the most serious phase that it has yet known in this country.

AN ENDOWED NEWSPAPER.

IN the retrospect of recent years there is no feature more significant than that offered by the benefactions of the philanthropically-minded wealthy. The immense sums of money devoted, whether by bequests or by gifts *inter vivos*, to charitable and educational purposes, give pause to cynicism and blunt the weapons of the socialist. There is some good in human nature, after all, and great fortunes are not an unmitigated social evil. The wealth thus diverted to beneficent ends may not always have been well-gotten, but its application, at least, is praiseworthy, and the act of its bestowal is a positive boon to society. We do not say that this atones for any possible dishonesty of acquisition; we do say that such bestowal may legitimately be considered as an isolated fact, and judged upon its own merits. Existing wealth, however acquired, is a positive power for good or evil; even if unfairly gained by its present owner, it is there, and must be reckoned with as a social factor. There are few cases in which an attempt to undo the injustice of the past, as far as injured individuals are concerned, would not be entirely futile. Had the late Jay Gould devised his estate to public purposes, it would have been ethical casuistry to frown upon the gift. If we may make this somewhat preposterous supposition, it cannot be denied that mankind would have been better off in consequence; nor can it be denied, on the other hand, that mankind would have been still better off had no such person lived. The benefaction and the personal account of the man who makes it present two distinct questions, which ought not to be, as they so often are, confused. It does not detract from the positive value of the one that the other leans heavily to the debit side of the balance.

This excursus has led us away from the original intention of our article, which was simply that of indicating a new outlet for the wealth of the philanthropist. We imagine that many a millionaire, disposed to liberality, has been deterred by lack of the imagination needed in the selection of a suitable object. To endow a church, or a hospital, or a college, must seem a hackneyed procedure, worthy as such institutions intrinsically are. To the millionaire of philanthropic velleity, in search of some comparatively novel method of benefitting his fellow-men, we would suggest the endowment of a newspaper. We can hardly conceive of a more civilizing influence than might be exerted, over a city and country, by a daily newspaper of ideal standards and aims, a newspaper dependent for support upon no political organization, no special group of commercial and industrial interests, no popular favor of any kind.

It may be taken for granted, in the present state of civilization, that no such daily newspaper would be likely to pay its own expenses. It is an admitted fact that the best intellectual or artistic activity needs to be supported. There are few exceptions to the rule that the best education, the best literature, the best scientific work, the best painting, sculpture, music, and dramatic art, cannot reward their producers as they should be rewarded. Architecture alone, among the higher works of the intellect, makes sufficient appeal to the practical instincts of men to be reasonably fruitful, and even the very best architecture must be done for glory rather than for pecuniary return. Still, in all these cases (dramatic art excepted), fame continues to supply the motive for good work, perhaps the best work that might in any case be hoped for. But the desire for fame alone, and the consciousness of doing work as it should be done, without thought of material profit, does not seem as yet to have been a motive sufficient for the production of anything like an ideal newspaper. At best, when the production is controlled by a single mind of sound instincts, the motive is mixed with more or less of commercialism; at worst, when the management is by a corporation, the money-getting motive is unleavened by anything better, and a newspaper is produced which has for its one object the enlargement of circulation by any means that do not overstep the limits imposed by the criminal law. That journalism has its ethics, that its exercise is a trust no less than the exercise of the legal, or medical, or teaching profession, or of the functions of public life, is a fact almost lost sight of in our modern scramble for wealth. How hopelessly blunted must be the moral sense of a man who can assume the office of a public teacher, in the wide sense permitted by journalism, with the deliberate intention of making it bring the largest possible returns, and who can unblushingly defend his course by pleading that the production of a newspaper is a business enterprise like any other.

The prevalence of this unethical spirit has produced the American newspaper of to-day, for which every intelligent American must blush. That certain features of excellence, mainly in the direction of prompt and comprehensive news-gathering, have been developed, is to be attributed rather to accident than to meritorious impulse. The American newspaper publisher has discovered that he can get rich by catering to the tastes of the vulgar, and vicious, and unlettered, and so snaps his fingers at clergymen, and teachers, and 'literary fellows' generally. Granting the immoral postulate from which he sets out, his course follows logically enough. The chief of our cities illustrates the two extremes of modern journalism, and the argument is commercially convincing. The best newspaper in the United States is published there, and also the worst; the circulation of each being inversely as its desert.

For this state of things public taste, considering only the verdict of numbers, is of course responsible, and offers a certain excuse for the policy of not setting too high a standard at once. What it does not excuse is the policy of arousing in humanity the dormant vulgarities and brutalities that civilization is slowly endeavoring to put to their final sleep, but that are still restless and wakeful. Many of our newspapers are engaged in this work of positive degradation, and for their diabolical activity no condemnation can be too emphatic. To the others, more or less self-convicted of time-serving, but still standing upon a mental plane slightly above that of the *homme sensuel moyen*, there is some faint praise to be given, at least of the sort that we give to the man who finds a pocket-book that he might keep undetected, and who restores it to the owner. It is, of course, only the barest decency to refrain from employing the worst methods of our worst journalism, but it is something to save even that relative form of virtue from the general wreck of worthy ideals.

It is because of these considerations; because most of our newspapers slight the real interests of civilized society for the sake of partisanship, vulgar personalities, and subjects that no healthy mind needs or cares to know very much about; because, in the words of the late Mr. Lowell, the press of the day 'is controlled more than ever before by its interests as a business rather than by its sense of duty as a teacher, and must purvey news instead of intelligence'; because, to sum it all up, the influence of such a press upon the national character must be incalculably bad, that we have made our serious suggestion to the ambitious millionaire. As an object-lesson in journalism, the existence in a community like New York or Chicago of a paper devoted to the real interests of the city and nation of its origin, uncontrolled by counting-room influences, able to keep its readers in touch with the best thought of the world, giving to art and science and literature their due prominence in its columns, unflinchingly standing for honest government and the purity of private morals,— the very existence of such a paper would mean much, although its readers should be outnumbered ten to one by those of lewd sheets of the baser sort. It could not fail in time to react upon the journalism of the country at large, and would offer a standing protest against the methods now current. It would steadily find its way into the family, and prove a potent influence in shaping the men and women of the future. Indeed, the most serious aspect of the present problem is that offered by the influence of newspapers upon the young. Upon this aspect the New York 'Evening Post' puts no undue emphasis when it says: 'The rising curiosity, which is in young people the most important instrument of mental growth, is not only turned wholly away from the serious and healthy side of American life, from sound politics, from wholesome literature, from art, science, industry, but is concentrated with hideous eagerness on the national sewers and pesthouses and dungheaps, until the whole of life becomes a filthy jest.' The endowment of a great newspaper, with suitable provision for its management by a body of highly educated, cultivated, and conscientious men, would prove a work of wider-reaching beneficence than the endowment of a great university.

IN MEMORIAM

CONSERVATION.

Aber der Erdgeist würde lächeln und sagen: 'Die Quelle, aus der die Individuen und ihre Kräfte fliessen, ist unerschöpflich und unendlich wie Zeit und Raum: denn jene sind, eben wie diese, Formen aller Erscheinung, Sichtbarkeit des Willens. Jene unendliche Quelle kann kein endliches Maass erschöpfen: daher steht jeder im Keime erstickten Begebenheit, oder Werk, zur Wiederkehr noch immer die unverminderte Unendlichkeit offen. In dieser Welt der Erscheinung ist so wenig wahrer Verlust als wahrer Gewinn möglich.'
— *Schopenhauer, W. a. W. u. V., III., 35.*

THEY pass away beyond the horizon's bourne
   That dimly rings us round; from out our view
   They vanish, starlike souls, nor any clue
Remains to track their orbits, and we mourn.
Life, once so fair, now of their glory shorn,
   Unbeaconed by their light, grows dark of hue,
   And sullen now the vault that erst was blue
Lowers, its radiance and its grace outworn.

Yet at our grief the Spirit of the Earth
But smiles, saying: 'To me are death and birth
   One thing; I dwell not in the world of space
   And time; my power is boundless to replace
What I destroy; then fear not any dearth
   Of stout torch-bearers in the soul's swift race.'

ALFRED TENNYSON.

IN the most memorable words ever written by a poet upon the subject of his art, Marlowe speaks of the unattainable ideal that still hovers before the poet's vision, whatever the beauty he may have succeeded in fixing upon the page, of the

> 'One thought, one grace, one wonder, at the least,
> Which into words no virtue can digest.'

By the critic, no less than the poet, this difficulty is felt when he seeks to digest into words the varied thoughts and emotions that have resulted from years of communion with the spirit of some great master of literature, when he endeavors to gather into the focus of concise expression all the wonder and the love, all the gratitude and the reverence, that have grown with the years, with the renewed study of familiar works, and with the fresh joy of acquaintance with new ones. But the delight that there is in praising (to use Landor's phrase), however inadequate the utterance, and the desire to bear some sort of witness to a spiritual influence that has chastened the passions and ennobled the ideals, often impels to speech where silence might be the fitter tribute.

It would indeed be difficult within these, or any reasonable limits, adequately to express Tennyson's claim upon the grateful remembrance of his fellow men, or to estimate, in other than the most general terms, the magnitude of the loss that has made this one of the most fatal months of the century. That he was the greatest English poet of his age is a fact so beyond the reach of cavil that it seems hardly worth taking the trouble to state. In the whole of English literature there are but the names of Shakespeare and Milton and Shelley worthy to be mentioned with his, and the literature of the world can add but few others to the list of such immortals. Tennyson was much more than the poet of the Victorian era, just as Virgil was far more than the poet of the Augustan age. The Englishman, like the Roman, was one of the few supreme masters of poetic expression, and in that fact is the assurance of an influence equally enduring. We may freely admit that he did not, like Pindar, soar to the empyrean, nor, like Dante, put upon record an age of human history; that he did not, like Shakespeare, sound all the depths of the soul, nor, like Hugo, control both the thunders and the lightnings. We may admit all this, but it still remains true that he gave a faultless expression to a wide range of noble thoughts; and no higher praise is known to literary criticism.

In the astonishing vitality of his genius, Tennyson stands alone among our great poets. From the publication of the volume of 1842 to this very year of his death — a full half-century — no other poetic force acting in our literature has been comparable to his. The work of his old age does not suffer in comparison with the work of his earlier years; we cannot point to any particular period of his life and say that he was then at his prime. The poet of the second "Locksley Hall" was as truly at his prime as the poet of the first. Indeed, there is about some of the late poems a beauty that seems almost unearthly, the evidence of a prophetic vision clarified by age, and placing him not only with the artists but with the seers. That 'Vision of the World' dimly revealed to his youth took ever with the advancing years an outline more defined, and his gaze penetrated more and more deeply into the heart of the universe.

> 'Upon me flashed
> The power of prophesying,'

sings his own Tiresias, and we cannot refrain from finding a personal utterance in the phrase, as well as in this other:

> 'But for me,
> I would that I were gathered to my rest,
> And mingled with the famous kings of old,
> On whom about their ocean-islands flash
> The faces of the Gods.'

The prayer has now been granted him; yet at this time of parting,

> 'When that which drew from out the boundless deep
> Turns again home,'

we cannot quite control our sorrow, or refrain from feeling that 'sadness of farewell' which he expressly urged should have no place in our hearts. The sense of loss is too recent and too great. In the calmer after-days, perhaps, we may remember that

> 'Men must endure
> Their going hence even as their coming hither,'

we may acquiesce in the view that 'ripeness is all,' and that Tennyson was ripe for death as few men ever are; we may take heart again when we think that

> The song that helped our father's souls to live,
> And bids the waning century bloom anew,'

is ours forever in all its imperishable beauty.

And how wonderfully rich and varied is the legacy that Tennyson has left us! Let us indicate a few of its more salient characteristics,—remembering all the while that in whatever aspect we view the poems, they constitute as a whole the most highly-finished body of work of like volume in our literature. In dealing with the facts of external nature, they show a minuteness and a delicacy of observation that cannot receive sufficient praise. Tennyson's skies and winds and seas, his mountains and fields, his trees and rocks, his birds and flowers, are described with unerring accuracy of sound and color and season. It has been the experience of many a reader of Tennyson to come upon some descriptive verse that has seemed at variance with ordinary observation, and afterwards to see exactly that aspect of nature revealed in fact. Mr. Swinburne offers an illustration of this experience. He is speaking of a verse of 'Elaine,'

'And white sails flying on the yellow sea.'
and says :

'I could not but feel conscious at once of its charm, and of the equally certain fact that I, though cradled and reared beside the sea, had never seen anything like that. But on the first bright day I ever spent on the eastern coast of England I saw the truth of this touch at once, and recognized once more with admiring delight the subtle and sure fidelity of that happy and studious hand. There, on the dull yellow foamless floor of dense discolored sea, so thick with clotted sand that the water looked massive and solid as the shore, the white sails flashed whiter against it and along it as they fled: and I knew once more the truth of what I had never doubted — that the eye and the hand of Tennyson may always be trusted, at once and alike, to see and to express the truth.'

Tennyson's intimate familiarity with the best literature of the world is conspicuous in his work, yet an uncritical reader gets but an imperfect idea of the poet's range among the classics of the past. So entirely has he made his own the thought of his predecessors, so complete has been the process of assimilation, that it would require a closer analytical study than has yet been made to indicate, with any kind of fulness, his indebtedness to others. And, of course, indebtedness in this sense ceases to be a real obligation, for it has always been the prerogative of genius to restate, in fresh and beautiful forms of expression, the world's older thought, thus giving it renewed currency and force. The work of illustrating this phase of Tennyson's genius is still to be accomplished, and will call for so rare a combination of scholarship and sympathetic insight that it may long remain undone. In a fragmentary way, it has been attempted, with provisional success, by a number of writers. Mr. Van Dyke's studies of 'Milton and Tennyson' and 'The Bible in Tennyson' are efforts in this direction. In the latter of these studies we read: 'The poet owes a large debt to the Christian Scriptures, not only for their formative influence upon his mind and for the purely literary material in the way of illustrations and allusions which they have given him, but also, and more particularly, for the creation of a moral atmosphere, a medium of thought and feeling, in which he can speak freely and with assurance of sympathy to a very wide circle of readers.' Mr. Van Dyke illustrates this thesis by many examples. Of Tennyson's debt to the Greek and Latin classics, much yet remains to be said. Such brief poems as the verses 'To

Virgil,' or the 'Frater Ave atque Vale,' inscribed to Catullus, might almost be made the subject of separate studies; and none but a profound scholar could unravel the close texture of the 'Lucretius,' and indicate the inspiration of its every phrase. Upon the idyllic side of his genius, Mr. Stedman has made a careful study of the relations between Tennyson and Theocritus, possibly attaching too much importance to this aspect of the English poet, yet doing his work with insight and thoroughness. But the study of what we may call Tennyson's allusiveness, or better, perhaps, his literary ancestry, has possibilities that are practically inexhaustible, and we may as well leave the subject at this point.

A word remains to be said of Tennyson's social and ethical ideals, of his philosophy of life. It has been too much the fashion to speak of him as merely reflecting the temper of the Victorian epoch. That he has done this is true enough, but it is also true that he has done much more than this. His outlook (at least since the 'In Memoriam' period) has extended far beyond the limits of his age, and has grown wider and wider with the advancing years.

'What hast thou done for me, grim Old Age, save
    breaking my bones on the rack?'

he asks in his latest volume of verse; and his answer is ready:

'I have climbed to the snows of Age, and I gaze at a
    field in the Past,
  Where I sank with the body at times in the sloughs
    of a low desire,
  But I hear no yelp of the beast, and the Man is quiet
    at last
  As he stands on the heights of his life with a glimpse
    of a height that is higher.'

The matter of his song is that which poetry has found fit in all ages, and the song reflects, not merely the aspirations of a race, but those of all mankind. The domestic affections and the sanctity of the home, a patriotism not narrowed into selfish disregard of other nations, and a religious feeling too broad to be fettered by any creeds, and too profound to be agitated by the surface currents of thought,—these are some of his themes. A conservative of the finest type, he was no reactionary, set upon barring the steps of progress. A champion of the existing order only as that order embodies the hard-earned fruits of the long struggle for light and justice, which is England's proudest title to a place in the foremost page of history, his eye was ever keen to perceive 'the vision of the world and all the wonder that should be,' and his mind ever alert in recognition of the fact that always, in any age not hopelessly stagnant, 'the old order changeth, yielding place to new.' The liberty which is not license, and the reasonable orderliness of life which accepts law without chafing, and which is alone made really possible by its acceptance of law — 'acting the law we live by without fear,' — this is the social ideal which he has persistently proclaimed for more than half a century. The lesson of 'Love and Duty,' that 'all life needs for life is possible to will,' and the lesson of the Wellington ode, —

> 'Not once or twice in our fair island-story,
> The path of duty was the way to glory:
> He, that ever following her commands,
> On with toil of heart and knees and hands,
> Thro' the long gorge to the far light has won
> His path upward, and prevail'd,
> Shall find the toppling crags of Duty scaled
> Are close upon the shining table-lands
> To which our God Himself is moon and sun,' —

are repeated again and again in his work, until we find them in 'Locksley Hall Sixty Years After':

'Follow you the Star that lights a desert pathway, yours
    or mine;
  Forward till you see the highest Human Nature is divine.
'Follow Light, and do the Right—for man can half
    control his doom—
  Till you find the deathless Angel seated in the vacant
    tomb.'

The picture of the poet's last hour will long remain engraved upon our memory. The midnight time, the full harvest moon streaming in over the Surrey hills and flooding the chamber with light, the august head, the features calm save for lips that murmured — what other words so fit? —

  'Fear no more the heat o' the sun,
    Nor the furious winter's rages,' —

the faces of the mourners stricken with grief and awe as that great soul faded 'into the unknown,' — nothing could have been more impressive; nothing could have added to the solemn pathos of the scene. 'Quiet consummation have' was doubtless the unspoken prayer of those who loved him best; of the other verse — 'And renownèd be thy grave' — thought need hardly have been taken; for England could offer nothing less to the poet so lately the greatest of her living sons, than a place beneath the arches of Westminster Abbey.

ERNEST RENAN.

WHILE the mortal remains of Tennyson found their final resting-place in the abode of England's mighty dead, the remains of Renan, provisionally interred in Montmartre, were but awaiting the necessary legislative action to be carried in state to the Panthéon. It was a singular fatality that simultaneously plunged both England and France into mourning, each for the greatest of its recent writers. For the position of Renan as the first Frenchman of letters after the death of Hugo was incontestable. And yet how different the paths by which the Frenchman and the Englishman attained immortality! The one addressed the world solely in verse; the other, exclusively in prose. The one reached truth by the intuitive processes of the poet; the other, by the minute and laborious investigations of the man of science. This, at least, is what the visible work of the two men reveals, yet perhaps the difference is not so great as it seems: perhaps it is to be largely explained by the fact that one chose to record both the operations and the results, while the other gave expression to the results only.

In Renan we see exemplified the highest type of the modern critical spirit, yet his work presents at the same time that nice balance of emotion and intellect too often destroyed by erudition. With him, neither history nor philosophy was allowed to grow arid, for the springs of feeling never ran dry. It is this that has given him a hold upon contemporary thought unshared by others of equal scholarship. He found the world of men intensely interesting, and he contrived to make his readers share the interest, however seemingly forbidding the gateway by which he approached the study of human affairs. It was by the gateway of philology that he chose to make the approach; but the philologist, in his view, must also be linguist, historian, archæologist, artist, and philosopher. Upon a foundation of the minutest and most conscientious study of philological details he built up the history of the past, and made it real to us because of the unfailing sympathies that went with the work, and because 'le vif sentiment des époques et des races,' the possession of which he attributed to Thierry, was at least equally his own.

The history, and especially the religious history, of primitive peoples was the principal subject of his study, and the great work to which most of his life was given was a history of the origins of Christianity, supplemented by a history of the people of Israel. This work he lived to complete in both parts; the first, in seven volumes, was finished many years ago; of the second, three volumes had appeared at the time of his death, and the remainder was ready for publication. We see, even in our own day, how much clerical antagonism is aroused by the scientific study of the history of Christianity; but the feeling excited thirty years ago, when the first part of Renan's great work was published, was far more general and more bitter than anything that has been witnessed of late. That first part was the famous 'Vie de Jésus,' a book having some slight faults of taste, but on the whole so beautiful and so reverent that we can only wonder at the bigotry which assailed it. 'Why do we write the life of the gods if not to make men love the divine that was in them, and to show that this divine lives yet and will ever live in the heart of humanity?' But clericalism was a force that had to be reckoned with in the France of 1863. It was only the year before, that, for a reference to Jesus of almost Apostolic reverence, contained in Renan's opening lecture as professor of Semitic languages at the Collège de France, his lecture-room had been closed by the government, to remain so, as far as Renan was concerned, for no less than seventeen years.

The religious intolerance that assailed Renan during the years of his early fame has not yet wholly subsided, although it has adopted of late more covert modes of attack, seeking to weaken his influence by discrediting his reputation as a scholar, or, exaggerating the sentimental side of his character, to suggest that he is not to be taken very seriously in anything. Matthew Arnold was, and is still, attacked in a very similar way by English orthodoxy, and, although his scholarship was not comparable with that of Renan, he was as clearly in the right upon all the essentials of the discussion. Both men possessed the art of being playfully serious; both had shafts of the keenest irony at their command; and both contrived to produce in their heavier-witted assailants the same sort of exasperation. Yet readers of 'Literature and Dogma' and 'God and the Bible' do not need to be reminded of how wholly Arnold's influence was exerted in favor of the religious temper and of genuine religious belief. How eloquently Renan has acted as the spokesman of religious feeling may be illustrated by many passages. He has the Voltairean weapons at his command, but he does not turn them against religious beliefs. 'Voltaire makes sport of the Bible,' he says, 'because he has no comprehension of the primitive productions of the human mind. He would have made sport of the Vedas as well, and should have made sport of Homer.' It is precisely the possession of the historic sense that gives to Renan's treatment of religion a seriousness that no one would now dream of attaching to Voltaire's. Here, for example, is a brief but weighty statement upon this subject:

'False when they seek to demonstrate the infinite, or to give it bounds, or to make it incarnate, if I may use the expression, religions are true when they affirm it. The gravest errors mingled by them with that affirmation count for nothing in comparison with the importance of the truth which they proclaim.'

And the following passage gives condensed expression to the whole of Renan's religious teaching:

'I have thought to serve religion by transporting it to the region of the unassailable, away from special dogmas and supernatural beliefs. When these crumble away religion must not crumble with them, and perhaps the day will come when those who reproach me, as for a crime, with making this distinction between the imperishable basis of religion and its transient forms will be glad to take refuge from brutal attacks within the very shelter that they have scorned.'

Like all men in whose psychical organization feeling has its full share, Renan was a man of moods, although not to so pronounced an extent as Carlyle and Mr. Ruskin. Like those English contemporaries a teacher in the highest sense of the term, he is also like them in the fact that his teaching does not present absolute consistency. Then the constant necessity of assuming points of view other than his own, forced upon him by the study of those primitive peoples to whose life and thought he gave the largest share of his attention, developed in him a certain form of the dramatic instinct, evidences of which may be found in his historical work no less than in the philosophical dramas of his later years. Both the facts above noted have been fruitful in misunderstandings, to say nothing of those other misunderstandings that always result from a dulness of perception in matters of the most refined literary art. To seize the exact shade of meaning is often essential to any sort of comprehension of Renan's work, and his irony is at times so delicate that a dull reader will often take it for sober earnest. It has been stated more than once, for example, that the tendency of Renan's teaching is towards a material and even sensual view of life. To one who has really penetrated his meaning and caught the essential spirit of his work as a whole, no judgment could be more grotesquely false than this. We have mentioned Carlyle, and in one point Renan's philosophy of life comes close to that of the Sage of Chelsea. What is the object of life? what its inmost purpose? Both men ask these questions again and again, and the answers of both are not dissimilar. Carlyle tells us many times that we have no right to happiness; that something far higher — namely, blessedness — should be the goal of our endeavor. When Renan exclaims, 'Il ne s'agit pas d'être heureux, il s'agit d'être parfait,' what is this but the same doctrine? Material well-being is indeed with most men a necessary condition for the realization of their higher selves, but it must never be taken as an end. Material ameliorations of the human lot 'have no ideal value in themselves, but they are the conditions of human dignity and the progress of the individual towards perfection.' Again he says: 'The wisdom of Poor Richard has always seemed to me a poor enough sort of wisdom.' Such a conception of life is simply immoral. 'What matters it to have realized, at the close of this brief life, a more or less complete type of external felicity? What really matters is to have thought much and loved much, to have looked with steadfast gaze upon all things, to dare criticise death itself in the dying hour.' And then, in one of those eloquent passages of which Renan was as great a master as ever put pen to paper, and that appeal so powerfully to the intellect because they enlist the emotions upon their side, he breaks into this beautiful rhapsody:

'Heroes of the unselfish life, saints, apostles, recluses, cenobites, ascetics of all ages, sublime poets and philosophers whose delight was in having no heritage here below;

sages who went through life with the left eye fixed upon earth and the right eye upon heaven; and thou above all, divine Spinoza, who chosest to remain poor and forgotten the better to serve thy thought and adore the Infinite, how much better you understood life than those who take it to be a narrow problem in self-interest, the meaningless struggle of ambition or of vanity! It had doubtless been better to make your God less of an abstraction, not set upon heights so dim that to contemplate him strained the vision. God is not alone in the sky, he is near each one of us; he is in the flower pressed by your feet, in the balmy air, in the life that hums and murmurs all about, most of all in your hearts. Yet in your sublime exaltation how much more clearly do I discern the super-sensual needs and instincts of humanity, than in those colorless beings upon whom the ray of the ideal never flashed, and whose lives from their first day to their last, were unfolded, precise and trim, like the leaves of a book of accounts!'

HIPPOLYTE ADOLPHE TAINE.

THE death of Taine took from the world a writer clearly the foremost among Frenchmen of letters after the loss of Renan. There are some, indeed, who would have claimed for him the highest place even during the lifetime of the great philologist and religious historian. For excellence of style, all would probably have conceded to Renan a higher place than to Taine, but for knowledge, for industry, for the orderly marshalling of facts, and for the exercise of a profound influence upon the thought of his age, one might have claimed with much show of reason that the author of 'Les Origines de la France Contemporaine' was of like stature with the author of 'L'Histoire des Origines du Christianisme.' Both men were brilliant exemplars of the scientific method in historical criticism, and both were singularly free from the spirit of provincialism that has characterized, in a notable degree, so many of the best French writers. In the work of the one as of the other, there is no more striking feature than its generous recognition of foreign, especially German, scholarship; than its catholic outlook upon the world of thinkers, and its readiness to accept the best that was offered, holding the Republic of the intellect to be an organization of more real and enduring significance that any political or racial group of the forces that make for solidarity among men.

As regards versatility, while it is possibly unfair to say that Taine had a wider range than Renan, it is still true that his activity found expression in a greater variety of forms. History, literature, philosophy, and art had in him an interpreter of insight and sagacity. In each of these fields he showed himself a master, and made important contributions to thought. We might almost mention travel as a fifth among these, for he was one of the keenest of observers, and the records of his sojourn in England, in Italy, and in the Pyrenees, belong to the small class of books of travel really instructive and of permanent value. That he kept active, even when at home, the faculty of the thoughtful traveller, is made evident by his 'Notes sur Paris.' In this book, disguised under the name of a certain M. Graindorge, he illustrated anew the objectivity of his critical standpoint, and earned for himself a gratitude not altogether unmixed.

The various manifestations of Renan's activity had philology for a starting-point, and his work was thus given the unity that comes from a fundamental subject common to its separate parts. 'The true philologist,' he said, 'must be linguist, historian, archæologist, artist, and philosopher at once.' The unity of Taine's work, on the other hand, is based upon method rather than upon subject. Few writers have ever developed so early, and kept so consistently in view, a distinctive method of critical investigation. His life-work was an endeavor to establish criticism upon a scientific basis, to provide it with axioms and postulates, to give it a certainty approximating to that of a mathematical demonstration. This endeavor was never absent from his work, whether it was engaged with ancient historians or modern philosophers, with Italian art or English literature, with the French life of to-day or the French life of the Revolutionary epoch. Taine's critical method has excited much controversy, and few have been willing to give it acceptance in its entirety. In its application, it broke down more than once, yet its fruitfulness is no less evident than the fact that it could not accomplish all that its author claimed. The tendency of modern criticism is unquestionably towards a scientific method; in history and philosophy it has already reached such a basis; that in art and literature it will eventually come to such a basis we may hardly doubt. Taine's work, whatever its shortcomings, moved with the main current of progress, and quickened that current in its flow.

Taine's work in art criticism is mainly contained in the five small volumes that were the immediate fruit of his professorship at the Paris 'Ecole des Beaux-Arts.' These books are delicate in style and penetrating in thought. They treat art, not as a matter of technique, but as a factor in the history of culture. The 'Voyage en Italie' also has many passages of the subtlest sort of art criticism. In philosophy, Taine made his *début* with a work upon 'Les Philosophes du XIXme Siècle en France,' an attack upon the *Philosophieprofessoren* that must have delighted Schopenhauer, if he chanced to read it. The impersonal subject of Taine's attack was eclecticism, the philosophical method — if we may call it a method — aptly described by one of Taine's biographers as ' that rhetorical spiritualism which in the eyes of the authorities had the advantage of giving no umbrage to the clergy, in the eyes of thinkers the disadvantage of tripping airily over the difficulties which it undertook to clear up and do away with, or else of evading them altogether.' Personally the attack was mainly upon Cousin, the leader of the eclectics, who took his revenge, some years later, by successfully opposing the bestowal of a special Academy prize upon the famous ' Histoire de la Littérature Anglaise.' Taine's principal philosophical work was his treatise ' De l'Intelligence,' characterized by himself as ' l'ouvrage auquel on a le plus réfléchi,' and published at a much later date than the one previously described. Although a quarter-century has elapsed since the work was written, and although the period has been one of remarkable activity in experimental psychology and philosophical criticism, the book remains one of the best and most instructive discussions of the subjects that we possess. Taine's philosophical standpoint is often stated as that of a follower of Hegel and Spinoza, but he has himself stated that his special indebtedness is rather to Montesquieu and Condillac.

It is in his treatment of literature that the peculiarities of Taine's critical method become most apparent. His first publication of any importance was a work on 'Lafontaine et Ses Fables,' and in this book we find fully developed his theory of race and environment as the essentially determining factors in literary production. In the 'Essai sur Tite-Live' these principles of criticism were applied a second time. They found their most thorough-going exemplification in 'L'Histoire de la Littérature Anglaise,' and the opposition they encountered has mainly taken this work as the objective point of attack. When Ste.-Beuve suggested that the work should have been called 'L'Histoire de la Race et de la Civilization Anglaises par la Littérature' he gave a succinct description of Taine's method. That method consists, when applied to the study of a whole literature, in analyzing the conditions of soil and climate under which the literature was produced, the prevalent political and social conditions that attended its development, and the ideal tendencies of the race that gave it birth. The method, in its application to the individual, takes further account of his special circumstances, of his ancestry, his place of birth, and his education, and of the particular tendencies of the age into which he was born. The whole, or nearly the whole, problem is one of heredity and environment; individuality, in the sense of spontaneous or incalculable manifestations of power, finds little place in this scientific system; genius, in whatever spiritual isolation it may seem to appear, is really the necessary product of forces whose origin we may trace and whose effects we may determine with considerable accuracy. This theory of literature, we need hardly say, has not met with general acceptance, in spite of the life-long advocacy given it by Taine. The persistence, the learning, and the eloquence with which he defended it have not proved convincing, although they have made it impossible for us wholly to ignore the factors whose influence upon literary production Taine believed to be paramount. To win acceptance, a scientific method must show itself productive of similar results when employed by many different observers, and it must fulfil the supreme test of enabling us to forecast the future with certainty. Tried by the first of these tests, the method has already been found wanting; that it will meet the second there is no good reason to believe. Whatever future the method may have will be found in its application to the general course of national literary developments. It will never foretell the individual manifestations of genius, as it never fully accounted for such phenomena as they occur in the past. For that task we shall need a deeper psychology than Taine, or any other thinker of the present century, has had at his command. But the fact that we cannot accept Taine's literary method should not prevent us from giving full credit to the many brilliant qualities of the work in which it had its most forcible expression. For Taine's work, with all its defects, is a better book than has yet been produced upon the whole of our literature by any one to the manner born. Every man has his limitations, and they sometimes appear most unexpectedly; in the finest of critical writing we come upon such grotesque vagaries as Taine's estimate of Tennyson, and Arnold's estimate of

Shelley. We accept these things as we do the spots on the sun's disc, and do not for that say that the light is but darkness. Had Taine been an English writer, we should have been surprised at the infrequency in his work of defective sympathies and untenable literary judgments. When we reflect that to know our literature he had first to learn our language, surprise gives place to wonder, and we think, not of the few cases in which he has failed to grasp the significance of our writers, but of the many whom he has discussed with penetrating sympathy and deep discernment. We think, for example, of his treatment of Swift, whom no critic, English or foreign, has better understood than he; we think of his treatment of the Elizabethan dramatists, and ask if it be possible that Voltaire lived but a century before.

The work of Taine's latest years will probably be accounted the greatest of his life. The writing of 'Les Origines de la France Contemporaine' was begun about twenty years ago. During that period we have had, at intervals of a few years, 'L'Ancien Régime,' dealing with the antecedent causes of the Revolution; 'La Révolution,' in three volumes; and the first of the two volumes in which the author proposed to deal with the Napoleonic period and its influence upon nineteenth century France. This great work is open to criticism on the score of its unfairness to the ideas and the leaders of the Revolution; it undoubtedly exaggerates the merits of the old order of things, and as undoubtedly fails in doing justice to the moral forces that made the Revolution triumphant for years, with all Europe armed against it. But in spite of these shortcomings the work gives us a more comprehensive array of facts and a more scientific sifting of evidence than has been given us by any previous historian of the subject. The legend of the Revolution can never again be what it was before Taine's merciless exposition of its intimate history. As for the Napoleonic legend, Taine has given that its *coup de grace;* he has put Napoleon upon record for the brigand that he was, and once for all voiced the sane judgment of posterity upon his character and his career. The concluding volume of this great historical work, left nearly finished at his death, was designed by the author ' to treat of the church, the school, and the family, describe the modern *milieu,* and note the facilities and obstacles which a society like our own encounters in this new *milieu*.' A dying man can have no greater consolation than the consciousness of having completed the work of his life; and it is pleasant to think that Taine's last hours, like those of Renan, were solaced by this reflection.

GUSTAV FREYTAG.

Gustav Freytag, who died at Wiesbaden, where he had lived in retirement since 1879, has been, on the whole, the most conspicuous figure in the German literature of the half-century now nearly ended, and of his contemporaries among belletristic prose-writers, not more than half a dozen — Reuter, Auerbach, and Scheffel among the dead, Herren Spielhagen, Heyse, and Dahn among the living — can claim a rank comparable with his. The life-work upon which his reputation rests was practically done during the quarter-century between 1855 and 1880, and of late years, although not wholly inactive, he has appeared a figure of the past rather than of the present. But his death seems none the less a shock, and his loss will be deeply mourned by the country of which he so honored the literature, and which stands to-day in greater need than ever of the social ideals inculcated by his works.

Freytag was born at Kreuzberg, in Silesia,

In Memoriam

July 13, 1816, thus living nearly to complete his seventy-ninth year. The son of a physician, he received his gymnasial training at Oels, and continued his studies at the Universities of Breslau and Berlin. Teutonic philology was his special subject, and his thesis for the doctorate, offered in 1838, was enitled 'De Initiis Scenicæ Poeseos apud Germanos.' The years 1839–1846 were spent at Breslau as a privat-docent. In 1847 he married a lady of rank and wealth, removed to Dresden, and shortly thereafter to Leipzig, where he engaged in the editorial conduct of 'Die Grenzboten.' His connection with this periodical was maintained (with an intermission from 1861 to 1867) until 1870. He had meanwhile (1867) become a liberal member of the Nord-Deutscher Reichstag. When the war of 1870 came, he joined the staff of the Crown Prince, and remained in the service up to Sedan. In that year also he became associated with the new weekly paper 'Im Deutschen Reich.' The loss of his wife in 1873, a subsequent marriage followed by a second bereavement, and his removal to Wiesbaden, constitute the remaining facts of external interest in his life.

Freytag's literary activity began during his years as a docent at Breslau, with a volume of lyrical poems, and four dramas — 'Die Brautfahrt,' 'Der Gelehrte,' 'Die Valentine,' and 'Graf Waldemar.' Two other dramas, 'Die Journalisten' (1854) and 'Die Fabier' (1859), complete the list of his writings for the stage, although in his 'Technik des Dramas,' published many years later, he was to do dramatic art an even greater service than that of producing so acceptable and healthful a stage-play as 'Die Journalisten.' This discussion of the principles of dramatic art, recently translated into English, is one of the most valuable of modern contributions to the subject with which it deals, and has the added weight of coming from a highly successful writer of plays.

Freytag's greatest work, the novel 'Soll und Haben,' well known to English readers as 'Debit and Credit,' appeared in 1855, and at once won for its writer the most cordial recognition from all discerning critics, although there were not lacking those who saw in the work the apotheosis of philistinism. Deliberately putting aside the romantic ideals of contemporary German novelists, the author of 'Soll und Haben' made of the merchant type the centre of interest, and the world of commerce that in which the scenes were laid. Realism of the good honest sort dominates this work, which depicts with unsurpassed fidelity the manners of a provincial town. Romantic elements, such as the episode of the Polish insurrection, are not lacking, but they are strictly subordinated to the controlling idea of the novel, which is that of rehabilitating in the eyes of the novel-reader those types of character which he is too apt to set lightly aside as prosaic, although they form the bone and sinew of every modern nation well advanced in the ways of civilization. That commercial integrity is as fine a thing as military glory, that the virtues of sobriety, patience, perseverance, devotion to the task at hand, and the performance of the humblest duties just because they are duties, are among the worthiest objects of endeavor—these are the lessons of the work, not too obtrusively inculcated, but everywhere underlying its structure. So genuine a piece of fiction is not often met with, or one that will so well bear scrutiny.

'Die Verlorne Handschrift,' published in 1864,

following the first novel at an interval of nearly ten years, is less obviously a masterpiece than 'Soll und Haben,' yet it must always occupy a high rank among the best products of German fiction. The story is that of a university professor, a large part of whose life is spent in the search for a manuscript of Tacitus, which he has reason to believe is still extant. His fate may be compared to that of Saul the son of Kish, for, while the manuscript eludes his pursuit, he finds instead, and wins for his wife, a very charming woman. The book abounds in admirable passages descriptive of life in a university town and at the court of a petty German prince. The author does not gild the commonplace as successfully as in 'Soll und Haben,' and his attempt to be humorous must be reckoned a distinct failure. On the other hand, the work abounds in fine, even eloquent, passages, among which the occasional characterizations of Tacitus are the most impressive. These, however, are the work rather of the essayist and historian than of the novelist, and our enjoyment of them has little to do with our interest in the story. The underlying purpose of 'Die Verlorne Handschrift' is the exaltation of the scholar's life, at the expense of more popular ideals, just as the purpose of ' Soll und Haben ' is the glorification — if we may use so strong a word — of the even less romantic life of the honest merchant. These two ideals, surely among the worthiest that can be urged, were and are peculiarly needed in Germany, where the unworthy ideals of militarism and the aristocracy are still opposed to them, and still have a stronger hold upon the nation than in most other civilized countries.

The books thus far enumerated, together with the series of ' Bilder aus der Deutchen Vergangenheit ' (1859–1862) and the biography of his friend Karl Mathy (1870), complete the list of Freytag's works up to the period of the War of 1870. The outcome of that conflict, so important to every German in its political significance, must be reckoned among the influences that shaped the literary activity of the novelist's remaining years. The most ambitious of all his undertakings is that of which the execution was begun soon after 1870, and which has represented the greater part of his literary activity since that date. It was during the course of the War that the plan of 'Die Ahnen' suggested itself to his mind, and the first person to whom the project was confided was the Crown Prince. The scope of the proposed work was thus defined in the dedication:

'This work is to contain a series of freely invented tales, in which are related the destinies of one family. It begins with ancestors of an early time, and shall (if the author retain his vigor and his interest in the work) be gradually brought down to the latest descendant, a hearty fellow who is now going about under the light of the German sun, without concerning himself very much about the deeds or trials of his forefathers. The book aims to contain poetic fiction,— and by no means a "history of culture."'

With these introductory words may be placed the other words appended to the last volume of the series:

'The author of "Die Ahnen" will be gratified if the reader will consider the work as a symphony, in whose eight parts a melodic theme is varied, carried out, and interwoven with others, in such a manner that all the parts, taken together, form a unit.'

The eight sections of 'Die Ahnen' were published in six volumes, between 1872 and 1880. The first volume, 'Ingo und Ingraban,' contains two episodes, both placed in Thuringia, and dealing respectively with the fourth and eighth centuries, with the Germanic struggle against Roman domination and the later struggle of the Franks against the encroaching Slavs. 'Das Nest der Zaunkönige' (1874) deals with the eleventh century and the reëstablishment of the imperial power by Henry II. 'Die Brüder vom Deutschen Hause' (1875) brings us to the thirteenth century, to the crusades, chivalry, and Frederick II. 'Marcus König' (1876) is concerned with the period of the Reformation. 'Die Geschwister' (1878) consists of two parts, 'Der Rittmeister von Alt-Rosen,' placed just after the Thirty Years' War, and 'Der Feldcorporal bei Markgraf-Albrecht,' placed in the times of Frederick William I. of Prussia. 'Aus einer Kleinen Stadt' (1880) brings us down to the Napoleonic invasion and the German national uprising of 1813. To this tale is added a 'Schluss,' in which the latest descendant of Ingo becomes a liberal editor and political idealist of our own times. German fiction has few works equal to 'Die Ahnen' in symmetry of plan and excellence of execution, and no student of the literature can afford to leave the series unread.

The temper in which Freytag wrote, not only 'Die Ahnen,' but his other books of fiction as well, may be illustrated by a 'thought' which he contributed as a sort of motto to the English translation of 'Die Verlorne Handschrift' made a few years ago. 'An efficient human life does not end upon earth with death; it persists in the disposition and acts of friends, as well as in the thoughts and activities of the nation.' This sense of the ideal continuity of soul-life is perhaps the main underlying motive of the best part of Freytag's work; a work, let us add, that everywhere appeals to the deepest and best instincts of our nature.

JOHN ADDINGTON SYMONDS.

THE death of Mr. Symonds, at Rome, has removed from the field of English letters one of its most graceful and accomplished representatives. He had only reached the age of fifty-two (Shakespeare's age), but his death was not wholly unexpected. Many years ago he was forced to leave England by pulmonary disease that threatened his life, and to take up a practically permanent residence at Davos, in the Engadine. His life in this mountain home has been described by himself in a number of charming magazine articles, and by his daughter in a recently published volume. He occasionally ventured upon short excursions from his seat of exile — mostly into Italy for the collection of the material required by his literary work — and it was upon one of these excursions that he gave up the long struggle with ill health.

His enforced residence in what was, for the literary worker, an almost complete solitude, has left its mark upon the work of his later years. Absence from all libraries but his own has given to much of that work an inadequate character, and left it lacking in the accuracy demanded by modern scholarship. For these defects, considering their excuse, he has been subjected to unfairly harsh criticism. It is really remarkable, under the conditions, that his work should have as high a scientific character as that with which it must be credited, and it surely offers a case in which the verdict of justice should be tempered by that of mercy. On the other hand, the author's long freedom from the distractions of English life enabled him to become a prolific worker, and the literary activity of his later years has been very marked. He has produced new volumes in rapid succession, and most of them have been volumes of unquestionable importance. Much of his later work has been shaped by the necessities of his isolated situation, and has taken forms that did not require the resources of great collections of material. His translations from the Italian, and his subtle analyses of the principles of æsthetic criticism, are illustrations of this general statement, although we must admit that the most important of his later works, the life of Michelangelo, had to be, and was, based upon an exhaustive study of the contemporary documents. As these were to be found in Italy, a country within his reach, he was enabled, even in his years of exile, to produce one work of capital scientific value.

Whatever form Mr. Symonds might give to his work, it was, like that of the great Frenchman whose loss we have so lately mourned, essentially critical in spirit, and its author will be remembered among the critics, rather than among the poets, the travellers, or the narrative historians. But his critical method was radically unlike that of his French contemporary, being as subjective as that of Taine was objective. He constantly sought to place himself within the mind of the writer or historical character with whom he was engaged, to see the world with his eyes, and to treat the environment as secondary in time if not in significance. Taine, as we all know, deduced the man and his work from the surrounding conditions; Symonds took the man and his work as the data of the problem, seeking to understand rather than to account for them. We are not here concerned to compare the two methods of work. Both of them are capable of excellent results, and either of them, if carried far enough, involves the other. It is sufficient to say that a writer committed to the one does not, as a rule, realize all the possibilities of the other, and falls short of that synthesis of the two that will produce the criticism of the future.

When Schelling spoke of architecture as frozen music, he sounded the keynote of what we may call the romantic manner in criticism. 'In romantic writing,' as we are told by Professor Sidney Colvin, 'all objects are exhibited as it were through a colored and iridescent atmosphere. Round about every central idea the romantic writer summons up a cloud of accessory and subordinate ideas for the sake of enhancing its effect, if at the risk of confusing its outlines.' To Mr. Symonds as a critic this definition of romanticism closely applies. A student of all the arts, a lover of natural no less than of man-created beauty, he was constantly bringing one set of impressions to the aid of another. He delighted in illustrating poetry by the phrases of landscape, and painting by the language of music. Those who will have only the clean-cut critical phraseology of Sainte-Beuve and Arnold resent the exuberance of Symonds, and do imperfect justice to its beauty as well as to its power of making a lasting impression. If they admit the latter quality, they will say that the impression is false, that the half-lights of romanticism are misleading, and that each artistic or other embodiment of beauty has its distinct province, forgetting that all forms of beauty appeal to the same emotional consciousness, and that the law of association is no less valid in the emotional than in the intellectual sphere. Professor Tyrrell, in a satirical sketch of the modern methods of classical study, says: 'To study the works, for instance, of the Greek dramatists is no longer a road to success as a scholar, or as a student. No: you must be ready to liken Æschylus to an Alpine *crevasse*, Sophocles to a fair avenue of elms, and Euripides to an amber weeping Phæthontid, or a town-pump in need of repairing.' This is clearly a reference to such books as Symonds's 'Studies of the Greek Poets,' and yet that book has done more to rouse an enthusiasm for Greek poetry, and foster a desire for its acquaintance, than all the unromantic tomes of the grammarians.

One subject Mr. Symonds made his own, and by his work done upon that subject he will be chiefly remembered. The Italian Renaissance has had historians of more minutely accurate scholarship, and its separate phases have perhaps found occasional treatment subtler and more profound than it was in his power to give them. But the period as a whole, its political and domestic life, its literature and art, received at his hands a treatment that lacks neither grasp nor sympathy, that is distinctly the best and most attractive in English literature. This treatment is chiefly embodied in the series of seven volumes, beginning with 'The Age of the Despots' and ending with the 'Catholic Reaction,' but is also to be sought in the masterly life of Michelangelo, in 'An Introduction to the Study of Dante,' in the verse and prose translations from Italian literature, and in the host of studies and sketches from time to time contributed to the periodicals. Upon the fascinating period with which all this work deals the best part of the author's thought was centred, and modern criticism offers few instances of so close an adaptation of a writer to his theme. Both by temperament and by training he was the man for the work, and the way in which, the main body of the work accomplished, he has lingered upon the outskirts of his chosen field of study reveals the extent to which the subject took possession of his mind and sympathies. The author's studies of other literatures than the Italian are chiefly represented by his work on the Greek poets, his essay on Lucretius, his 'Sidney' and 'Shelley' in the 'English Men of Letters' series, his 'Jonson' in the series of 'English Worthies,' and his thick volume entitled 'Shakespeare's Predecessors in the English Drama,' intended to be the first volume of a complete history of our great dramatic period. His volumes of travel in Italy and Greece are genuine literature, exemplifying the wealth of his learning, the justness of his perceptions, and the beauty of his style. His original verse, considerable in amount, falls short of being great poetry, but may be read with keen pleasure, and appeals strongly to the reflective mind. His essays on the principles of æsthetics are burdened with verbiage and not always lucid in enunciation, but they are weighty enough amply to repay their readers. When we consider his work as a whole we are impressed with its range, its sanity, and its devotion to the Goethean ideal of the good, true, and beautiful. His death has made a conspicuous vacancy in the rapidly thinning ranks of our older writers, and upon no other shoulders does his particular mantle seem yet to have fallen.

CHRISTINA GEORGINA ROSSETTI.

ONE of the closing days of 1894 was saddened by the death of Miss Rossetti, the youngest of that famous quartette of brothers and sisters of whom Mr. W. M. Rossetti is now left the sole survivor. Maria Francesca, who died in 1876, was the oldest of the four, having first seen the light in 1827. Then came Dante Gabriel in 1828, William Michael in 1829, and Christina Georgina in 1830. Miss Rossetti gave early evidence of her poetic talents, as is shown by the privately-printed volume of 'Verses' dated 1847. In 1850, with her brothers, she wrote for the famous 'Germ,' over the pseudonymous signature of 'Ellen Alleyne.' It was not, however, until 1862 that she took her destined place among the greater Victorian poets, with 'Goblin Market and Other Poems.' That volume was followed, in 1866, by 'The Prince's Progress and Other Poems,' and, in 1881, by 'A Pageant and Other Poems.' It is upon the contents of these three collections that Miss Rossetti's reputation must rest, although she did a considerable amount of other literary work. Before discussing the character of her poems, we may dispose of the other books by a simple enumeration. 'Commonplace and Other Short Stories' (1870) and 'Sing-Song: A Nursery Rhyme-Book' (1872) are titles that speak for themselves. 'Speaking Likenesses,' a volume of 'quasi-allegorical prose,' and 'Annus Domini: A Prayer for Every Day in the Year,' both bear the date 1874. 'Seek and Find,' 'Called to the Saints,' and 'Letter and Spirit,' three religious works in prose, date from 1879, 1881, and 1883, respectively; while 'Time Flies,' a reading diary in alternate verse and prose, appeared in 1885, and was, we believe, her last published volume. These devotional books, which have both found and deserved a large and appreciative audience, are distinctly out of the common, but the spirit which finds expression in them finds utterance still more intense and rapturous in the three volumes of song to which we now turn.

It is not the least of the glories of English poetry that two women should be numbered among the singers whom we most love and honor. It is perhaps idle to inquire whether Mrs. Browning or Miss Rossetti is to be esteemed the greater poet; the one thing certain is that no other English woman is to be named in the same breath with them. These two stand far apart from the throng, lifted above it by inspiration and achievement, and no account of the greater poetry of our century can ignore them. If there is something more instinctive, more inevitable in impulse, about the work of Mrs. Browning, there is more of restraint and of artistic finish about the work of Miss Rossetti. The test of popularity would assign to the former the higher rank, just as it would place Byron above Keats and Coleridge, or above Wordsworth and Shelley; but the critic has better tests than the noisy verdicts of the multitude, and those tests lessen, if they do not quite do away with, the seeming disparity between the fame of the two women.

The longer pieces which introduce Miss Rossetti's three volumes are not the most successful of their contents. It is rather to the lyrics, ballads, and sonnets that the lover of poetry will turn to find her at her best. Who, for example, could once read and ever forget such a sonnet as ' Rest '?

> ' O Earth, lie heavily upon her eyes;
>   Seal her sweet eyes weary of watching, Earth;
>   Lie close around her; leave no room for mirth
> With its harsh laughter, nor for sound of sighs.
> She hath no questions, she hath no replies,
>   Hushed in and curtained with a blessed dearth
>   Of all that irked her from the hour of birth,
> With stillness that is almost Paradise.
> Darkness more clear than noonday holdeth her,
>   Silence more musical than any song;
> Even her very heart hath ceased to stir:
>   Until the morning of Eternity
>   Her rest shall not begin nor end, but be;
> And when she wakes she will not think it long.'

Or who could escape the haunting quality of such a lyric as this:

> ' When I am dead, my dearest,
>   Sing no sad songs for me;
> Plant thou no roses at my head,
>   Nor shady cypress-tree;
> Be the green grass above me
>   With showers and dewdrops wet;
> And if thou wilt, remember,
>   And if thou wilt, forget.

> 'I shall not see the shadows,
>   I shall not feel the rain;
> I shall not hear the nightingale
>   Sing on, as if in pain:
> And dreaming through the twilight
>   That doth not rise nor set,
> Haply I may remember,
>   And haply may forget.'

The poem just quoted can hardly fail to recall, in feeling, thought, and measure, Mr. Swinburne's 'Rococo,' and thus emphasizes the spiritual relationship of the author to the poets of the group sometimes styled ' Pre-Raphaelite.' Similarly, the perfect lyric called 'Dream-Land' is clearly akin to 'The Garden of Proserpine,' and it is not difficult to discern the same sort of kinship between Miss Rossetti's 'Up-Hill' and Mr. Swinburne's 'The Pilgrims.' Now the point to be noted is that all three of Miss Rossetti's poems were published in the volume of 1862, while the three Swinburnian poems date from several years later. There is, of course, no question of imitation — in each case what remains a simple theme with the one poet is elaborated into a symphony by the other — but it is difficult to escape the conclusion that the man was influenced by the woman in all three of the cases. Particularly with 'Up-Hill' and 'The Pilgrims,' we note the common use of the dialogue form and the absolute identity of the austere ethical motive.

Miss Rossetti's verses sometimes suggest those of other poets, but we always feel that her art is distinctly her own. The divine simplicity of Blake is echoed in such a stanza as

> 'What can lambkins do
> All the keen night through?
> Nestle by their woolly mother,
> The careful ewe.'

The melting, almost cloying, sweetness of the Tennysonian lyric meets us in these verses:

> 'Come to me in the silence of the night;
> Come in the speaking silence of a dream;
> Come with soft rounded cheeks and eyes as bright
> As sunlight on a stream;
> Come back in tears,
> O memory, hope, love of finished years.'

As for the influence of the great Italian, which shaped so powerfully the thought of every member of the Rossetti family, it is less tangible here than in the work of her greater brother, yet to it must be attributed much of the tenderness and the pervasive mysticism of her poems. It is perhaps most apparent in the two sonnet-sequences, 'Monna Innominata' and 'Later Life,' both included in the volume of 1881. And the influence of that brother who bore the sacred name of the Florentine is likewise intangible but pervasive. We get a glimpse of it in 'Amor Mundi,' for example, and in many a *vanitas vanitatum* strain. But we must repeat that Miss Rossetti's genius was too original to be chargeable with anything more than that assimilation of spiritual influence from which no poet can hope wholly to escape, and which links together in one golden chain the poetic tradition of the ages.

If in most of the provinces of the lyric realm Miss Rossetti's verse challenges comparison with that of our greater singers, it is in the religious province that the challenge is most imperative and her mastery most manifest. Not in Keble or Newman, not in Herbert or Vaughan, do we find a clearer or more beautiful expression of the religious sentiment than is dominant in Miss Rossetti's three books. In this respect, at least, she is unsurpassed, and perhaps unequalled, by any of her contemporaries. In her devotional pieces there is no touch of affectation, artificiality, or insincerity. Such poems as 'The Three Enemies' and 'Advent' in the first volume, 'Paradise' and 'The Lowest Place' in the second, and many of the glorious lyrics and sonnets of the third, will long be treasured among the religious classics of the English language. Perhaps the poet's highest achievement in this kind is the 'Old and New Year Ditties' of the first volume. Some such claim, at least, has been made by no less an authority than Mr. Swinburne for the closing section of the poem.

'Passing away, saith the World, passing away;
Chances, beauty, and youth sapped day by day;
Thy life never continueth in one stay.
Is the eye waxen dim, is the dark hair changing to gray
That hath won neither laurel nor bay?
I shall clothe myself in Spring and bud in May:
Thou, root-stricken, shalt not rebuild thy decay
On my bosom for aye.
Then I answered: Yea.

'Passing away, saith my Soul, passing away;
With its burden of fear and hope, of labor and play;
Hearken what the past doth witness and say:
Rust in thy gold, a moth is in thine array,

In Memoriam

A canker is in thy bud, thy leaf must decay.
At midnight, at cock-crow, at morning, one certain day
Lo, the Bridegroom shall come and shall not delay:
Watch thou and pray.
Then I answered: Yea.

'Passing away, saith my God, passing away:
Winter passeth after the long delay;
New grapes on the vine, new figs on the tender spray,
Turtle calleth turtle in Heaven's May.
Though I tarry, wait for Me, trust Me, watch and pray.
Arise, come away, night is past, and lo it is day,
My love, My sister, My spouse, thou shalt hear Me say.
Then I answered: Yea.'

It is peculiarly fitting that the author of these fervid and solemn verses, written for one New Year's season, should herself have passed away on the very eve of another.

JOHN TYNDALL.

LOOKING over the death-roll of 1893, we are more than once reminded of Lear's terrible fatalism :

> 'As flies to wanton boys are we to the gods,
> They kill us for their sport.'

Freeman, hardly beyond his prime, found his death in a Spanish inn, the victim of a pox-infected mattress. Symonds, with many fruitful years seemingly before him, was taken off by a cold that passed into pneumonia, while returning from the last of his Italian journeys. To Tschaikowsky, on a visit to St. Petersburg, death came in a pestilential draught of water, and cholera marked him for its own in the fulness of his powers. Last of all, and most ironical in its accent, came word that John Tyndall was dead, but from no blow dealt by the legitimate assailants of mortality. An overdose of chloral, given by the fatal error of a loving wife, cut short his career, prematurely, we must say, although the best of his work was doubtless accomplished.

Professor Tyndall occupied a large place in English scientific thought, and the vacancy caused by his death will not easily be filled. His original researches resulted in important contributions to knowledge, especially in the domain of molecular physics. Although they do not place him in the first rank of nineteenth century Englishmen of science, they secure for him a high position in the second. He belongs with Professor Huxley and Lord Kelvin, rather than with Darwin and Maxwell. He had the German training, and he combined the German thoroughness with the English instinct for systematic and perspicuous presentation. Great as was his service in the character of an investigator, he did a still greater service to his countrymen in the character of an expositor. What Professor Huxley did for the new biology created by Darwin, was done by Professor Tyndall for the new physics created by Joule and Faraday and Maxwell. It is customary in certain quarters to sneer at popular science; and there is not a little popular science, so-called, which justifies the attitude of contempt. But no such reproach attaches to the work of men like Tyndall, whose knowledge of the subjects with which he dealt was both thorough and accurate. It is difficult to estimate the full value of the work done for the advancement of English public opinion in matters of science by the group of writers to which Tyndall belonged, and of which his death left Professor Huxley the most distinguished remaining representative. They came at just the right time, and they brought just the right kind of powers to their task. Without the labors of these men, the great nineteenth century revolution in physical and biological science would indeed have been, none the later, a *fait accompli;* but it would have taken much longer to reach the popular consciousness.

Professor Tyndall stood in the vanguard of the revolutionary forces, and bore the brunt of the battle. Twenty years ago, he incurred the *odium theologicum* by an article in 'The Contemporary Review,' proposing that the efficacy of prayer should be subjected to a scientific test. He little thought, good easy man, what a hornets' nest this cold-blooded suggestion would bring about his ears. When, in the year following this incident, he was presented at Oxford for the honorary doctorate, he found his candidacy bitterly opposed by one of the professors of divinity in the University, on the ground that his teachings contravened 'the whole tenor of that book, which with its open page inscribed *Dominus illuminatio mea* the University still bears as her device.' Only a year later than this, his address before the Belfast meeting of the British Association, in which address he professed to discern in matter 'the promise and potency of every form and quality of life,' again aroused his theological opponents, and fanned afresh the flame of their zealous indignation. Only three or four years before these occurrences, Professor Huxley, in a lecture upon Descartes, speaking of the religious persecution of which that philosopher was a victim, had said: 'There are one or two living men, who, a couple of centuries hence, will be remembered as Descartes is now, because they have produced great thoughts which will live and grow as long as mankind lasts. If the twenty-first century studies their history, it will find that the Christianity of the middle of the nineteenth century recognized them only as objects of vilification.' The vilification to which Tyndall was subjected, in consequence of the acts above alluded to, came as a prompt and striking new illustration of Professor Huxley's remark.

Most earnest men, watching the world from day to day, get impatient because it moves so slowly. And yet, looking back over a few years, the same men will find cause for astonishment at the rapidity of its advance in this nineteenth century of ours. The Copernican doctrine required from one to two centuries to make its way; the Darwinian doctrine accomplished an equal revolution of thought in one or two decades. The suggestions that seemed so startling when made by Tyndall twenty years ago would to-day hardly cause a ripple of excitement anywhere. Few intelligent people, whatever their religious beliefs, are now shocked at the admission of spontaneous generation as a necessary link in the evolutionary chain, and few of them hold to a doctrine of prayer that invites such tests as that proposed by Tyndall in the early seventies. Of recent years, Tyndall has been assailed by the politicians almost as vehemently as he was once assailed by the theologians, and time will bring him a justification similar to that which it has brought him in the earlier controversy. In his denunciation of the recent Gladstonian attempt to dismember the United Kingdom he joined himself with such men as Tennyson and Matthew Arnold, and his memory need fear no defeat in that alliance.

The noble intellectual temper of the man that has just died, the bent of mind which we venture to call essentially religious in spite of the religious antagonisms which it evoked, and the eloquence of expression that he knew how to impart to the subjects which so deeply concerned him, may most fittingly be illustrated by the closing paragraph of the famous Belfast Address:

'And now the end has come. With more time, or greater strength and knowledge, what has been here said might have been better said, while worthy matters here omitted might have received fit expression. But there would have been no material deviation from the views set forth. As regards myself, they are not the growth of a day; and as regards you, I thought you ought to know the environment which, with or without your consent, is rapidly surrounding you, and in relation to which some adjustment on your part may be necessary. A hint of Hamlet's, however, teaches us all how the troubles of common life may be ended; and it is perfectly possible for you and me to purchase intellectual peace at the price of intellectual death. The world is not without refuges of this description; nor is it wanting in persons who seek their shelter and try to persuade others to do the same. I would exhort you to refuse such shelter, and to scorn such base repose — to accept, if the choice be forced upon you, commotion before stagnation, the leap of the torrent before the stillness of the swamp. In the one there is at all events life, and therefore hope; in the other, none. I have touched on debatable questions, and led you over dangerous ground — and this partly with the view of telling you, and through you the world, that as regards these questions science claims unrestricted right of search. It is not to the point to say that the views of Lucretius and Bruno, of Darwin and Spencer, may be wrong. Here I should agree with you, deeming it indeed certain that these views will undergo modification. But the point is, that, whether right or wrong, we claim the right to discuss them. The ground which they cover is scientific ground; and the right claimed is one made good through tribulation and anguish, inflicted and endured in darker times than ours, but resulting in the immortal victories which science has won for the human race. I would set forth equally the inexorable advance of man's understanding in the path of knowledge, and the unquenchable claims of his emotional nature which the understanding can never satisfy. The world embraces not only a Newton, but a Shakespeare — not only a Boyle, but a Raphael — not only a Kant, but a Beethoven — not only a Darwin, but a Carlyle. Not in each

In Memoriam

of these, but in all, is human nature whole. They are not opposed, but supplementary — not mutually exclusive, but reconcilable. And if, still unsatisfied, the human mind, with the yearning of a pilgrim for his distant home, will turn to the mystery from which it has emerged, seeking so to fashion it as to give unity to thought and faith, so long as this is done, not only without intolerance or bigotry of any kind, but with the enlightened recognition that ultimate fixity of conception is here unattainable, and that each succeeding age must be held free to fashion the mystery in accordance with its own needs — then, in opposition to all the restrictions of materialism, I would affirm this to be a field for the noblest exercise of what, in contrast with the *knowing* faculties, may be called the *creative* faculties of man. Here, however, I must quit a theme too great for me to handle, but which will be handled by the loftiest minds ages after you and I, like streaks of morning cloud, shall have melted into the infinite azure of the past.'

This fine peroration, which we have quoted in its entirety, serves better than a volume of comment to explain the influence which Tyndall has exerted upon his contemporaries, and especially upon the younger generation. The scientist of the dryasdust type may scoff at it as mere rhetoric, but it has stirred many of its readers as with a trumpet-call to steadfastness and honesty of purpose in the pursuit of truth. The power to write in this fashion, backed by the power to employ the most rigorous of scientific methods in his own researches, made of Tyndall one of the most vital of the directive intellectual forces of his age, and brings to his memory a host of mourners who early caught the contagion of his spirit, and have sought to follow in his footsteps.

THOMAS HENRY HUXLEY.

THE death of Professor Huxley came not without warning, and he had to his account the exact scriptural tale of a man's years. A worker and a fighter all his life, the pen was in his hand when overtaken by the illness that was to prove fatal in the end, and he was replying, with unabated vigor of expression and force of logic, to the latest attack made by mysticism upon that stronghold of reasoned and ordered knowledge which we call science, and of which he had for nearly half a century been one of the doughtiest of defenders.

In the popular consciousness, indeed, Huxley ranked among the leading representatives of English science, probably as the foremost among them after the death of his old-time colleague, John Tyndall. It may be worth while to consider for a moment what this estimate means. There is practically no such thing, in the present age of the world, as the representation of science by any one man. Aristotle was perhaps the only man for whom, in any age, that distinction may be claimed. Nowadays, a man can represent science only by representing biology, or physics, or geology, or something even narrower than these. Huxley represented English science in the sense that he gave a large part of his life to the subject of comparative anatomy, and made some fairly important contributions to our knowledge of that subject. But his work was not comparable to that, in their respective subjects, of such men as Faraday, or Lyell, or Maxwell, to say nothing of Darwin. It was good work, without doubt, but it was equalled by a score of Englishmen of his own generation, and surpassed by a respectable number.

But the average person, when he thinks of Huxley as a scientific leader, recks little of his comparative anatomy, and has probably never heard of the great work on 'Oceanic Hydrozoa,' the manuals of vertebrate and invertebrate anatomy, or even the monograph on 'The Cray-Fish.' It is a very different sort of work that has given Huxley his immense reputation, the work which, for the most part, may be found in the nine volumes of his 'Collected Essays,' and which is, of its kind, almost unparalleled in our literature. These volumes, it is true, have a great deal to say about science — biological science in particular — but they announce no original investigations worth speaking of, and they are not contributions to scientific knowledge in any strict sense. Some will dismiss them with a sneer, as mere popularizations, as a sort of juggling with other men's ideas. This contemptuous procedure, it need hardly be said, gets no sympathy from us, and it is as distinctly wrongheaded as the attempt, already discussed, to classify such books as 'Man's Place in Nature' and 'The Physical Basis of Life' among important scientific works.

Wherein, then, lies the value of these nine volumes of essays, if it is inadequate to consider them as mere popularizations, however skilful, and quite wrong to call them contributions to science? We should say that the first and most important claim to be made for them is that they reveal a strong philosophical thinker; that beneath their graceful rhetoric and acute dialectic there is a method of fundamental importance, clearly conceived, and rigorously applied to the special subject, whatever it may be, under consideration. What that method is may be seen plainly enough in any one among half a dozen of the more formal discussions; most plainly, perhaps, in the noble essay, dated 1870, upon the 'Discours de la Méthode' of Descartes. Indeed, the author recognized the principle above stated as constituting the unifying element in his seemingly so diversified work when he gave to the initial volume of the revised edition of the 'Essays' the significant title 'Method and Results.' And this title might have been made to cover the whole collection, for we find, whether the subject of an essay be 'Man's Place in Nature' or 'Evolution and Ethics,' the story of the Gadarene swine or the organization of the State, that the discussion always proceeds upon well-defined lines, and with close reference to a controlling organon. It was no vagary, as some of his readers thought, when he turned from his anatomical studies to write for the 'English Men of Letters' a philosophical analysis of the work of Hume; it was rather an indication of the real bent of his mind, which always looked beyond

In Memoriam

the half-unified knowledge of science to the fully-unified knowledge that we call philosophy.

The healthy English mind is not distinguished by an aptitude for metaphysics, and Huxley's mind was distinctly of the healthy English type. He was content with a method, when a Frenchman or a German would have been satisfied with nothing short of a system. Hence, he was willing to leave many of the questions of philosophy unanswered, content to carry his method as far it would go, and to admit ignorance of the regions beyond. He even coined a word with which to name this philosophical attitude, and the immediate adoption and currency of that word showed that it met a long-felt want. Since it came into our circulation, agnosticism, like many other words, has been used as a counter by wise men and as a full-weight coin by fools, but it has justified itself, on the whole, as a useful addition to our philosophical terminology.

The lectures and writings of our arch-agnostic have, during the past forty years, aroused a good many religious antagonisms; some of these have become allayed by time, and some are still active. It took a bold Englishman in the sixties to champion the Darwinian doctrine of descent and to combat the grotesque Miltonic theory of creation; but Huxley was never lacking in courage, and he bore without flinching the brunt of theological attack and vilification. The world—that is, all the world worth considering—came round to his side sooner than could have been anticipated by a student of the history of new and fruitful ideas—of their long hard struggle with ignorance, and blindness, and all the banded legions of the old order of thought—and the last score of years left to the stout-hearted philosopher were serene with the satisfaction of complete achievement in at least one important field of his endeavor. But the theory of creation was not the only stronghold occupied by the popular theology of his fellow-countrymen, and, when that was battered down, there were others to be attacked. All these assaults were not, of course, directed against religion at all, any more than were the Voltairean assaults of a century previous, and the *infâme* that Huxley sought to crush in the world of thought was as little deserving of consideration as was the engine of political and social despotism which Voltaire's memorable and magnificent crusade did so much to demolish. We should say that Huxley, far from being an enemy of religion, was one of the best friends it has ever found, and we have no doubt that, from the more enlightened twentieth-century religious point of view, he will be remembered as such.

For our part the aspect of Huxley's life and work that compels the deepest gratitude is the absolute honesty by which that life and that work were characterized throughout. One does not need to accept all of his conclusions to admire the intellectual process by which they were reached. His logic may now and then have been at fault, but it scorned every species of sophistical subterfuge. To get at the truth, not merely to make a better-sounding argument than his opponent, was always his aim. He hated shams as Carlyle hated them, but, instead of inveighing at them with stormy prophecy ('I am not equal to the prophetical business'), he employed the better weapon of compactly-wrought argumentation. Very recently, taking a retrospective view of his life, he made this statement of what had been its aims and its guiding principles:

'Men are said to be partial judges of themselves.

Young men may be, I doubt if old men are. Life seems terribly foreshortened as they look back, and the mountain they set themselves to climb in youth turns out to be a mere spur of immeasurably higher ranges when, with failing breath, they reach the top. But if I may speak of the objects I have had more or less definitely in view since I began the ascent of my hillock, they are briefly these: To promote the increase of natural knowledge, and to forward the application of scientific methods of investigation to all the problems of life, to the best of my ability, in the conviction, which has grown with my growth and strengthened with my strength, that there is no alleviation for the sufferings of mankind except veracity of thought and action, and the resolute facing of the world as it is, when the garment of make-believe by which pious hands have hidden its uglier features is stripped off. It is with this intent that I have subordinated any reasonable, or unreasonable, ambition for scientific fame which I may have permitted myself to entertain, to other ends; to the popularization of science; to the development and organization of scientific education; to the endless series of battles and skirmishes over evolution; and to untiring opposition to that ecclesiastical spirit, that clericalism, which in England, as everywhere else, and to whatever denomination it may belong, is the deadly enemy of science.'

It is a noble *apologia pro vita sua*, and the world will not readily forget what it owes to this man's single-hearted devotion to truth. His tombstone should bear the inscription, *Veritatem dilexi*, that Renan asked to be cut upon his own, and the measure of his delight in the truth should be the measure of posterity's delight in cherishing his memory.

OLIVER WENDELL HOLMES.

THE last of the famous group of New Englanders who made the dream of American literature a fact, the last man of letters to survive from that *annus mirabilis* which also gave to America Lincoln and Poe, to England Tennyson and Darwin, Oliver Wendell Holmes has stolen peacefully to his rest, and we have indeed broken with the past. Few lives have meant so much to Americans as that now ended, its years so nearly those of the century which it adorned. As the intellectual associates of the gentle Autocrat went to their own places one by one, the affection in which they were held seemed to be transferred to the ever-lessening group of those who yet remained, until, in concentration of grateful recollection, it was all heaped upon one beloved head. Now, there remain but memories to which we may cling; the last leaf has fallen from 'the old forsaken bough,' and we smile, as he bade us do, but through our tears.

The love which Americans have felt, and always will feel, for the group of our distinctively national poets, including Bryant and Longfellow, Whittier and Lowell, besides the one whose loss we now mourn, has had few parallels in other nations for either depth or sincerity. We knew that they were not great poets, as the world measures poetic greatness; we knew that their voices were not of those that for all ages speak to all mankind; but they have had for us so many endearing associations, their names have been so indissolubly linked with whatever was best and noblest in our history and our aspirations, that we could not wholly measure them by the cold standards of objective criticism. The indigenous nature-lyrics of Bryant, Longfellow's delicate treatment of the romantic aspects of American history, the passion that fired Whittier's songs of freedom, and the ethical fervor and downright manliness to which Lowell gave such varied utterance,—all these things meant something to us, something very precious, very personal, and altogether incommunicable to the alien. So we did not mind it very much when the amiable foreign critic told us that most of our poets were either mocking-birds or corn-crakes. We knew that it would be useless to explain or to remonstrate; we knew, in fact, that his language and his tests were not ours, nor ours his.

The work of Holmes, besides having qualities peculiarly its own, shares also in the special appeals indicated above. There is no lack of lyrical or romantic effect, of patriotic or ethical passion, in the long series of volumes that began with the 'Poems' of 1836 and ended with 'Before the Curfew' in 1888. And how much there is that falls without the categories thus summarily designated!

> 'What shapes and fancies, grave or gay,
>   Before us at his bidding come!
> The Treadmill tramp, the One-Horse Shay,
>   The dumb despair of Elsie's doom!

> 'The tale of Avis and the Maid,
>   The plea for lips that cannot speak,
> The holy kiss that Iris laid
>   On little Boston's pallid cheek!'

And then Holmes was so much more than a mere singer. The very fact that we most frequently call him the Autocrat rather than the poet suggests something of his versatile ability.

With one aspect of his life-work we are not here concerned. As a medical practitioner, as a teacher of anatomy, and as a writer in the special field of his profession, he had a full and honorable career, and we may fancy that he more than once said to the physician Holmes, This is what I really am, the rest is trifling; just as Lamb said of his India House folios, 'These are my real works.'

But we may put all this aside, and the man of letters remains, not sensibly diminished in stature. For to his credit stand many entries. There are the three novels, and of them we must say that they have few equals in our American fiction. 'A Mortal Antipathy' we might perhaps spare, but we would not willingly lose 'Elsie Venner,' even if science frown upon its thesis, or 'The Guardian Angel,' even if it do not in all respects fulfil the requirements of the fictive art. We should say that no reservations need be made when it is a question of praising the four volumes of Table-Talk, which begin with the breakfast-table and end with the tea-cups. And besides these gifts, he gave us the sympathetic and beautiful memoirs of Motley and Emerson, and the many prose miscellanies that are only less charming than his more famous works.

As a poet — and in the final settlement the poet will outweigh the writer of prose — Holmes preserved for us the spirit of the classical age at a time when romanticism was in full cry. But, as Mr. Stedman happily suggests, his work was a survival rather than a revival. It is curious, indeed, as the same acute critic remarks, to note how persistently he remained an artificer upon the old-fashioned lines, although ever alert to seize the new occasion and the new theme. We have had no other so expert in personal and occasional verse, no other who could so distil the very quintessence of Yankee humor, or of the other and finer qualities of the New England intellect, into the most limpid of song. And when he was entirely serious, how exquisite was his touch, how pure his pathos, how clear his ethical sense! Let 'The Voiceless,' 'Under the Violets,' and 'The Chambered Nautilus' bear witness. And, since no one knew so well as he the word most fit to be spoken upon any solemn occasion, let us write in his own words his epitaph:

In Memoriam

'Say not the Poet dies!
   Though in the dust he lies,
He cannot forfeit his melodious breath,
   Unsphered by envious death!
Life drops the voiceless myriads from its roll;
   Their fate he cannot share,
   Who, in the enchanted air
Sweet with the lingering strains that Echo stole,
Has left his dearer self, the music of his soul!

'He sleeps; he cannot die!
   As evening's long-drawn sigh,
Lifting the rose-leaves on his peaceful mound,
   Spreads all their sweets around,
So, laden with his song, the breezes blow
   From where the rustling sedge
   Frets our rude ocean's edge
To the smooth sea beyond the peaks of snow.
His soul the air enshrines and leaves but dust below!'

WILLIAM FREDERICK POOLE.

IN the death of Dr. Poole American history lost one of its best equipped and most painstaking students, the profession of librarianship one of its foremost exponents, and 'The Dial' one of its stanchest friends and most valued contributors. Although he had made his home for some years past in the university suburb of Evanston, a few miles from Chicago, his work was done in the latter city, which for twenty years reckoned him among its most distinguished citizens. The number of persons who, in this great community, are identified with intellectual rather than with material interests is still relatively so small that the disappearance from our midst of so commanding a figure as that of Dr. Poole is a public loss more grievous than it would be in many other places. His death leaves a social vacancy not easily to be filled, even from the public point of view; from that of the friends who have loved and honored

In Memoriam

him for so many years, the mere suggestion of its ever being filled is a mockery.

William Frederick Poole was born at Salem, Massachusetts, December 24, 1821, thus being at the time of his death seventy-two years of age. The annals of his career may be briefly chronicled. He entered Yale College in 1842, and was graduated in 1849. This period includes an interregnum of three years spent in earning the money needed to complete his college education. President Timothy Dwight, of Yale University, was one of his classmates. From the time of graduation from college to the close of his career, the story of his life, viewed externally, is little more than a statement of the various libraries that he was called upon to direct or to organize. He was an assistant librarian in the Boston Athenæum from 1850 to 1852; Librarian of the Boston Mercantile Library from 1852 to 1856; Librarian of the Boston Athenæum from 1856 to 1869; and Librarian of the Cincinnati Public Library from 1869 to 1874. Called, in 1873, to the work of organizing the Chicago Public Library, he entered upon that task early in 1874, and remained at the head of the Chicago institution until 1887, when he was called upon to undertake the task of organizing the reference library endowed by the late Walter L. Newberry, of Chicago, and known by the name of its generous founder. During the nearly seven years that he lived to act as the director of that institution, he collected for its uses nearly one hundred thousand volumes, and lived to superintend their transfer to the magnificent new building which is to be the permanent home of the Library.

Librarianship, in this country, has during the past twenty years become one of the learned professions; that it has become so is due in very great measure to the efforts of Dr. Poole. To secure for his fellow-workers the recognition accorded to the clergyman, the lawyer, and the physician; to substitute the trained bibliographer for the mere custodian of books; to establish professional schools of librarianship; to make the public familiar with the principles of rational library architecture; to facilitate access to collections of books, and to enlarge their usefulness by library helps prepared by the coöperation of bibliographers — these were, briefly stated, the aims towards whose accomplishment he devoted, for a full half-century, an exceptionally active and industrious life. He was a member of the New York Convention of Librarians held in 1853, the first convention of the sort ever held anywhere. He helped organize the American Library Association in 1876, was one of the Presidents of that body, and attended all but one of its annual meetings. He represented this country at the first International Conference of Librarians, held in London in 1877, and was, in 1893, at the head of the World's Congress Auxiliary Literary Congresses, one of which was an International Congress of Librarians. The papers published by him upon professional subjects are very numerous, but are difficult of access. These papers ought to be collected, for they contain much material of permanent value.

As a librarian, Dr. Poole's methods were characterized by sagacious practicality and clear common sense. He mistrusted the elaborate scientific systems now in vogue with our younger bibliographers — systems which are excellent for the uses of the librarian, but sadly perplexing to most of the people for whom libraries are collected. His methods of classification and catalogue-making were to a certain extent empirical, and not a little is to be said on behalf of empiricism in such matters. He never lost sight of the fundamental principle that books are meant to be used; that their chief end is not attained when they are catalogued and shelved. He wanted the public to use the books under his charge, and encouraged such use in many ways. He welcomed the work of University Extension, and tried to make the public library a helpful adjunct to that work. And long before University Extension was talked about in this country, he sought to bring the school into more intimate relations with the library, and arranged for bibliographical talks to students, illustrated by the literature of the subjects talked about.

Such a collection of Dr. Poole's bibliographical papers as we have suggested would be a worthy monument to his memory. But a still worthier monument already exists in the shape of the great 'Index to Periodical Literature.' The author began this important work as a student, when he was acting as librarian of a college society. Its first edition was printed in 1848, making an octavo of 154 pages. In 1853 it reappeared in an octavo of more than three times the thickness of the earlier volume. In 1882 (the author having meanwhile secured the coöperation of a number of his fellow-librarians) it made its third and final appearance, again multiplied threefold as to the number of pages, and much more than that as to the quantity of matter. Two supplements have since been published, with the coöperation of Mr. W. I. Fletcher, bringing it down to 1892.

As a student of history, Dr. Poole devoted himself chiefly to subjects connected with the early settlement of this country. His 'Anti-Slavery Opinions before 1800' is a valuable contribution to the history of the 'peculiar institution' in America. His paper on 'The Popham Colony' discussed certain conflicting claims between Maine and Massachusetts as to priority of settlement, deciding in favor of the latter. He investigated the history of the Northwestern Ordinance and the connection therewith of Manasseh Cutler, making himself the recognized authority upon that important subject. He pricked the bubbles of the Pocahontas story and of the Mecklenburg Declaration so effectively that they were relegated to the realm of myth, and are not likely again to find serious defenders. He published valuable studies in the history of the early Northwest. Most important, perhaps, of all his studies were those relating to early Massachusetts history, and especially to the Mathers and the subject of witchcraft. These subjects were assigned to him in 'The Memorial History of Boston,' and were frequently discussed by him elsewhere. He did much to correct the erroneous popular estimate of Cotton Mather, showing him to have been learned, sagacious, and tolerant, free from responsibility for the witchcraft delusion, and a commanding figure worthy of the respect and admiration of posterity. In this, as in other instances, Dr. Poole, himself a descendant of the Puritans, stoutly defended his ancestors against the misrepresentations under which they have suffered. Another piece of historical work, possibly the most important done by him, was his lengthy historical and critical introduction to the reprint of Captain Edward Johnson's 'Wonder-Working Providence of Sion's Saviour in New England.' These numerous historical studies, no less than those devoted to the professional work of the librarian, are so scattered as to be difficult of access, and richly deserve collection and publication in permanent form.

Many of Dr. Poole's historical papers were contributed to the journal upon which now devolves the sad task of paying a tribute to his memory, and it was through his good offices that the contents of 'The Dial' were, from the start, included in the great 'Index.' The first number of 'The Dial' appeared in May, 1880, and the first article in that number was a review, by Dr. Poole, of the new edition of Hildreth. His latest contribution, which was probably the last piece of work done by him, was a vigorous defense of the Puritans of which our readers will hardly need to be reminded. Between these two contributions, upwards of thirty others from his pen appeared in the pages of 'The Dial'; contributions devoted, almost without exception, to subjects in American history. Whatever might be his subject, the forcible and picturesque qualities of his style could not fail to be impressive, and the pages that he wrote, however aggressive and tending to excite opposition, always held the attention, and were never invaded by anything remotely suggestive of dulness.

The bibliographer and the historical student combined in William Frederick Poole were known to the world; something better than these, the man himself, was known to his friends. The brusqueness of his manner, at first a little repellant to those who came into contact with him, was soon seen to be but the outward expression of a mental habit of the rarest sincerity. And upon those who had the privilege of his intimacy was made the impression, dominant above all others, of his absolute integrity, intellectual and moral. They realized that here was a man who simply could not think one thing and say another, or swerve by so much as a finger's breadth from what he believed to be the right course, were the matter in question great or small. Such men are none too common in the world, and when one of them leaves it, his place, for those who have really known him, is not likely to be filled again.

Lightning Source LLC
Chambersburg PA
CBHW031948230426
4367 2CB000010B/2093